POETS
AGAINST
THE WAR

Edited by Sam Hamill
with Sally Anderson and others

THUNDER'S MOUTH PRESS/NATION BOOKS
NEW YORK

POETS AGAINST THE WAR
Copyright © 2003 Poets Against the War
Introduction © 2003 Sam Hamill

Published by
Thunder's Mouth Press/Nation Books
161 William Street, 16th Floor
New York, NY 10038

Nation Books is a co-publishing venture of the Nation Institute
and Avalon Publishing Group Incorporated.

Library of Congress in Publication Data is available.

ISBN 1-56025-539-0

9 8 7 6 5 4 3 2 1

Book design by Paul Paddock
Printed in the United States of America
Distributed by Publishers Group West

For Laura Bush

CONTENTS

Introduction

"We suffocate among people who think they are absolutely right, whether in their machines or their ideas. And for all those who can live only in an atmosphere of human dialogue, the silence is the end of the world."—Albert Camus

"A patriot is not a weapon. A patriot is one who wrestles for the soul of her country
as she wrestles for her own being, for the soul of his country . . ."
—Adrienne Rich

When I was invited to a White House symposium on poetry by Laura Bush, I asked a few fellow poet-friends to send me poems speaking "for the conscience of our country," in opposition to George Bush's plans for a "Shock and Awe" attack on Baghdad that would result in about 3000 missiles hitting the city in the first two days of war. How could I have known I had 11,000 friends? Between the last week of January and the end of February, poetsagainstthewar.org became host to several historic moments: Never before in recorded history have so many poets spoken in a single chorus; never before has a single-theme anthology of this proportion been assembled; never before had such wide-reaching national—and eventually global—"Days of Poetry Against the War" been organized. A historic moment indeed. Besides the sheer quantity and enthusiasm of 11,000 poets, we have brought poetry into the American consciousness as never before, reminding our citizenry that poetry (and all the arts) indeed addresses social and historical subjects.

I learned only after sending off my request for poems that the subjects of Mrs. Bush's gathering were to be Walt Whitman, Langston Hughes and Emily Dickinson, three of the most original and anti-establishmentarian poets in our literature. Once the White House got wind of our plans, the symposium was promptly "postponed." Mrs. Bush's spokeswoman said, "While Mrs. Bush respects the right of all Americans to express their opinions, she, too, has opinions and believes it would be inappropriate to turn a literary event into a political forum." So much for "Poetry and the American Voice" at this White House. I hadn't even had time to decline the invitation.

My wife, Gray Foster, and our friend, Nancy Giebink, had volunteered to download and format what we thought would be a few hundred poems, but by late the second day, the email address we had given out was totally overwhelmed. We were saved by Andy Himes and friends at projectalchemy.org, a Seattle-based group of techno-wizards who, moved by our cause, set up our website. Within a few days, we had twenty-five editors down-loading poems as they poured in at a rate of one per minute. If the Bush people thought canceling the poetry symposium would quell the rising tide of voices joining Poets Against the War, they must have been shocked, if not awed, by the response. Poets will not be silenced.

On February 12, 2003, the day the original White House symposium was scheduled, there were over 200 "poetry readings against the war" held throughout the country. In the midst of a blizzard on February 17, Avery Fisher Hall in

New York's Lincoln Center was filled nearly to capacity for a second round of readings, sponsored by the antiwar organization, Not in Our Name. A boisterously enthusiastic crowd cheered four generations of poets, including Galway Kinnell, Saul Williams, Stanley Kunitz, Sapphire, Arthur Miller and others. Poetry, its traditions and its role in culture was discussed in news stories, on op-ed pages and in the streets as perhaps never before in our nation's history.

On March 5, in the company of fellow writers W. S. Merwin, Terry Tempest Williams, and Emily Warn, along with Poets Against the War board member Peter Lewis, I presented to Ohio Congresswoman Marcy Kaptur an electronic manuscript containing 13,000 poems by nearly 11,000 poets. It took a ream of paper to print just the names of contributors in three columns of small type. Ms. Kaptur spoke eloquently of the need for "right words" in our struggle to save our country from becoming a rogue nation. Congressmen Jim McDermott, Dennis Kucinich, and John Conyers also expressed gratitude and encouragement.

Can 13,000 poems inhibit this or any administration planning a war? It is only one step among many. But it is an important step, as each is. We join physicians against the war, teachers against the war, farmers against the war, and others. Poets Against the War helped bring about hundreds of poetry readings and discussions around the world while compiling a document of historic proportion. And when our critics on the right suggest that poetry might somehow divorce itself from politics, we say, "Read the Greeks, read the classical Chinese; tell it to Dante, Chaucer, Milton or Longfellow. Tell it to Whitman, Dickinson or Hughes. Tell it to Garcia Lorca, to Joseph Brodsky or to the Chinese poets living in exile in our country today." The voice of dissenting poets is unwelcome at this White House, but it has been and will be heard.

Mussolini defined fascism as the marriage of the corporation and the state. When a handful of conglomerates clutch virtually the entire media, repeating the official party line hour after hour, we approach a fascist state. A true patriot is born in the act of questioning and in acting upon a reasoned response. Poetry, too, is born in an act of questioning. Since most poets write in the same language politicians are given to abuse, in the language of everyday common speech, they must struggle to reveal clarity by way of musical and imagistic expression, and by transparency of emotion. We question ourselves, our art and certainly those who rule. And through a miraculous marriage of intuition and scholarship, we are "given" poetry to write. "A hero," the Greek Nobel prize-winning poet George Seferis wrote, "is one who moves forward in the dark."

One of the great questions poets face today is just how we carry our traditions into a world of "pre-emptive war," while remaining true to our obligation to assay the human condition from an intensely personal, often subjective perspective. Sloganeering accomplishes nothing. Nor do we, 11,000 poets, hold a single notion of a proper solution. We agree only in our mutual opposition to an immoral war of American aggression. We write and teach, nurse and cook, sell insurance, wash dinner dishes and change diapers, our art and our hearts heavy with grieving. As poets, as citizens of this one world. In war, it is always the innocent who suffer most.

I do not believe, as some have said, that "poets are the conscience of our country." I believe that they are a conscience, each by each, and I also believe there are things learned from poetry that can be learned no other way. Poetry is a source of revolution from within. It leads us to question, to meditation.

With the aid of Sally Anderson and a volunteer team of some two dozen editors, I have selected fewer than two hundred poems to represent our collective voice. There are, no doubt, innumerable jewels still to be found in the vaults of poetsagainstthewar.org. American poetry in the last century has been among the greatest of the last millennium, and many of its finest poets are included here: W. S. Merwin, Adrienne Rich, Maxine Kumin, Carolyn Kizer, Galway Kinnell, and others. There are also contributors who may be publishing for the first time, or nearly so. There are black and white and Hispanic and Asian-American poets, few of whom would have been anthologized just a hundred years ago. Our poetry, like our culture, has been deeply enriched by the politics of emancipation, the politics of civil rights and gender equality, and by cultural cross-pollination especially.

Laura Bush called off her symposium on "Poetry and the American Voice." It is my privilege to offer in its stead this single-theme anthology of living American voices. These are the voices of our poets; they come from every segment of society. And if they form a single chorus in opposition to a war, they also celebrate our country by expounding a compassionate view of the universe. A government is a government of words, and when those words are used to mislead, to instill fear or to invite silence, it is the duty of every poet to speak fearlessly and clearly.

—SAM HAMILL
March 2003

Virginia Adair

90 YEARS OLD
CALIFORNIA

*I was a teacher for years, and have had three books of poetry published.
I have been blind for many years. My first book was published when I
was in my 80s.*

Casualty

Fear arrived at my door
with the evening paper
Headlines of winter and war
It will be a long time to peace
And the green rains

———

Kim Addonizio

48 YEARS OLD
OAKLAND, CALIFORNIA

Author of five books, including Tell Me, *a National Book Award
finalist in 2000.*

Cranes in August

They clutter the house,
awkwardly folded, unable
to rise. My daughter makes
and makes them, having heard
the old story: what we create
may save us. I string

a long line of them over
the window. Outside
the gray doves bring
their one vowel to the air,
the same sound
from many throats, repeated.

———

Lucy Adkins

52 YEARS OLD
LINCOLN, NEBRASKA

I grew up in rural Nebraska, attended the University of Nebraska, and received my B.S. in Secondary Education with an emphasis in English from Auburn University. My poems have appeared in publications such as Plainsongs, Nebraska Territory, Midwest Quarterly Review, The Owne Wister Review, *among others, as well as in the anthologies* Woven on the Wind *and* Times of Sorrow/Times of Grace.

Geese, October 2002

Night,
walking in and out of streetlight shadows,
kicking leaves along Sheridan Boulevard,
down Winthrop,
and then I hear them.
Geese! Flying high above the city,
their geese voices
calling through the clouds and mist
calling out yellow to the tops of the cottonwoods

calling out red sumac, burning bush
chrysanthemums in whites, fuchsias, blood red orange—
and tonight the fog like smoke,
rose-tinged and strange
in city lights.

Overhead, the geese are flying the good flight
they have flown for thousands of years
north to the nesting grounds,
wild hearts singing.

Fifteen hundred miles east,
our country's leaders
are voting for war,
voting yes to bombs and fire
and poison gas,
yes to armies marching across the sand;
But here in Lincoln, Nebraska
the geese fly over
the old wisdom in their feathers,
their sinew,
their good hollow bones.
They call through the clattering leaves, the fog.
Listen,
yes, listen!

Fawzia Afzal-Khan

44 YEARS OLD
NEW YORK

Pakistani-American scholar, professor, poet, memoirist, classical singer, actor, wife, mother of two. Author of two books: Cultural Imperialism and the Indo-English Novel *and* The Pre-Occupation of Post-colonial Studies, *as well as countless scholarly and political essays, poems, nonfiction.*

Billy Bush Sam-ton

Osama
Sam A
Uncle Sam

will you
defend me
against that SOB
who fondled my breasts
and squeezed my ass

he said Lie
through your tongue
baby it's okay

you're defending the
integrity of your
Man
-ly Nation hood
Not
hoodwinking but

upholding the
Truth (of)
Justice
Law
Democracy

That's why
it's okay
to nukefry
those damn boys
in Af-ghan-is-tan
and Su-dan
I-raq
and I-ran

barbarian chauvinists
not like us oh no
MONIKA

don't be disappointed
I've vindicated your
Honor
see by striking
those afroasian Breasts

so very different from
your soft White ones
I am a
Real Man now
are you Proud
of Me

Kelli Russell Agodon
KINGSTON, WASHINGTON

Kelli Russell Agodon's poems have appeared in the Rattapallax, Seattle Review, Parnassus, Crab Creek Review, The Adirondack Review, *and other publications. Recently, she was nominated for two Pushcart Prizes and awarded a writing residency at Soapstone Writers Retreat in Oregon. Kelli is an Artist Trust GAP recipient for her manuscript "Beginning to Speak." Currently, she is the Poetry Editor for the online literary journal* Margin *and a Regional Coordinator for the United Poetry Coalition (formerly Poets for Peace). She lives in a small seaside community outside Seattle with her husband and daughter.*

Of a Forgetful Sea

Sometimes, I forget the sun
sinking into ocean.

Desert is only a handful of sand
held by my daughter.

In her palm,
she holds small creatures,
tracks an ant, a flea
moving over each grain.

She brings them to places
she thinks are safe:

an island of driftwood,
the knot of a blackberry bush,
a continent of grass.

Fire ants carried on sticks,
potato bugs scooped
into the crease of a newspaper.

She tries to help them
before the patterns of tides
reach their lives.

She knows about families
who fold together like hands,
a horizon of tanks moving forward.

Here war is only newsprint.

How easy it is not to think about it
as we sleep beneath our quiet sky,
slip ourselves into foam, neglectful
waves appearing endless.

———

Robert Aitken

Gatha

When people talk about war

I vow with all beings

to raise my voice in the chorus

and speak of original peace.

Francisco X. Alarcón
CALIFORNIA

Alarcón teaches at the University of California at Davis. He has published eleven books of poems. He is also an award-winning author of bilingual books of poems for children. He is currently a finalist for poet laureate of the state of California. His most recent book is From the Other Side of Night / Del otro lado de la noche: New and Selected Poems.

Pathetic Lines/Pobres versos

what do we gain
writing
the saddest
lines
tonight

using ink
so bitter
it makes
tissue
out of paper

when they
scoff and
jeer at us
their arms
covered with blood

———

qué ganamos
con escribir
los versos
más tristes
esta noche

usar la tinta
más amarga
hasta hacer
pañuelo
el papel

cuando ellos
se burlan
de nosostros
con sus armas
ensangrentadas

———

Joan Aleshire
64 YEARS OLD
CUTTINGSVILLE, VERMONT

January 2003; Vermont

Two to three feet
west of the Greens—
on the radio, not news:
snow rising to the sills,
road losing its way in drifts.

Maple logs crumble in the stove,
glow, go black;
the red pot hisses with steam.
The cats stretch out on anything
in print, wanting me to read them
as closely as the news.

Self-sufficiency, smugness—
It could be a hundred years or two
before, when the house was new,
except for this brighter light,
and words traveling on night air
from nerve centers of knowing:
news of coming war, and fear
that clogs the engines of power,
makes them run rough:

THE POST reports the CIA
sends terror suspects to countries
where torture is normal—

What kind of torture,
the host holds his even tone,
might these countries employ?
Oh, shocks to the genitals,
hanging by the thumbs, rape—
Anyone will say anything,
just to stop the pain.

What country has ours become?

If war is forced upon us,
another voice says, the one
who is forcing it, huffing
like the wolf that will blow
all of our houses down—
the one I don't listen to.

Here, with hand-hewn beams,
warmth, light, good neighbors beyond,
it's almost possible to believe
the old virtues abide, as if outside
this snow globe, the trees didn't sigh
and creak in the wind from the south,
in distress and resistance. As if
under the snow, this beautiful land
weren't cracking. Breaking in two.

Annette Allen

48 YEARS OLD
SIDNEY, INDIANA
I work as an Information Systems engineer. I am studying creative writing at Creighton University.

On His Way to Kuwait

One evening after work, standing around his desk,
talking about everything and nothing, in other words
about life, he said, "The children are spoiled, they have
no purpose. They live to spend money. They understand
nothing. Little savages. What they need is a war to whip
them into shape. To give them some depth, some real
understanding of the meaning of life."

I was shocked. Perplexed, my ear had heard,
". . . to give them some death, some real
understanding of the meaning of life."

I shut down that conversation fast, like a machine
in some factory that had hold of someone's hands,
tearing off the fingers while co-workers looked on
in horror. I left for the day. We never discussed it again.

Last week at lunch, sitting in a booth at our favorite
vegetarian restaurant, I asked him how things were
going. He spoke of his mother, who is dying, and his
sisters, who have their troubles, and his youngest
son, who is graduating from high school in the spring.

I noted lavender half moons of fatigue under his eyes.
In them I saw him sleepless, standing at his living

room window, keeping endless watch on a silent
  suburban
street. "And Philip?" I asked after the only member
of his family he had not mentioned. His firstborn, who
enlisted in the Marines on September 10th , 2001.

"Philip is on his way to Kuwait," he said most casually.
"In a day or so he'll be camped within sight of the Iraqi
border." We both looked down at the table, sipped our tea.
An old conversation hovered in the air between us, filled up
the silence with something hard and bitter. I kept to myself
the question that was on my lips and I pray with my every
breath it is never answered.

Alise Alousi
37 YEARS OLD
*Detroit poet and writer-in-residence. Iraqi-American. This poem first
appeared in* Dispatch Detroit, *volume 5.*

What to Count

What does it mean to hold your mouth to another's ear.
  What does it mean to make something stealth. Where
  do
you feel it. Where do things happen when they happen
  on a train.

A shelter that falls in on itself. A hospital that can't help
you, a pencil without lead. Are there things you could
use.

A whisper what does it excite in you. She said stand on the
corner with a sign should I? Something falling soft in
the air tiny disappear your skin damage with a capsule.
It is a good way to eat all the time. He doesn't want the
numbers in the bag—100. 150. 200. 250. 300. Women,
children, the old only.

What matters is that you are innocent when you die like this.

Step into the flash. Remember this day. Don't throw rice
for birds, a bubble you catch in your teeth. Smile's not
right. The scent behind your ear makes his head hurt.

Sent home crying when the visitors come through hands
in pockets and chewing gum and pencils and penicillin
and. taking notes. bombs dropped last week didn't
they. In the school yard. Where are your dual—use
shoes?

What counts is the circle when you dance like this.

Up out of the water too much chlorine in the backyard
pool, see it in their eyes. Children. Looking into the
sun.
What is on the other side.

They say we can't fill the order not even one drop on a
hot stone. Nothing will be clean or white again. The
xray

of your wrist, chest, lungs will be done by hand come
    back in seven hours. There are too many young men
    they
will die of general malaise right in the street and there is
    one ambulance in the city and there is nowhere for it
to take you.

What counts when you fall like this, is the way they lift
    you, bending at the knees.

Salih Altoma (translator)

73 YEARS OLD
INDIANA UNIVERSITY, BLOOMINGTON, INDIANA
*Professor emeritus of Arabic and comparative literature at Indiana
University. Altoma has translated a number of Iraqi poems dealing
with the Gulf War and its tragic consequences. Below is a poem by
Salam al-Asadi (1936-1994), an eyewitness to the bombing of his
hometown in southern Iraq. He died as a refugee.*

The Clay's Memory

       by Salam al-Asadi,
       translation by Salih Altoma

The night is a descending myth
a forest of black snow
a sky of mud spitting out its mute ashes all over
thus we appear as a blend of tears and dust

no distinction between our children's frightened eyes
and the palm trees' wounds
or between the silence of the schools' empty classrooms
and
the Euphrates' sad rumbling
no difference between the bitter gasp, the sigh of
withering souls,
the trees' smoke, the planes' thunder,
and the veils of drowned women floating on the river's
surface
like numbed shivering black spots
the river that was stunned by the disaster,
a storm that swept all things into a bottomless abyss
the howl of the planets, rubble, haggard faces, bewil-
dered eyes, agitated palm trees,
and the bowels of the dead, children's corpses,
and sparrows trembling against closed horizons.

Julia Alvarez

VERMONT

I am an author of four novels, poems, essays, children's books, among them How the García Girls Lost Their Accents, In the Time of the Butterflies, *and most recently,* Before We Were Free *(for young adults). Along with my husband, Bill Eichner, I run a sustainable farm/literacy project in my native country, the Dominican Republic. Currently, I am also a writer in residence at Middlebury College.*

The White House Has Disinvited the Poets

The White House has disinvited the poets
to a cultural tea in honor of poetry
after the Secret Service got wind of a plot
to fill Mrs. Bush's ears with antiwar verse.
Were they afraid the poets might persuade
a sensitive girl who always loved to read,
a librarian who stocked the shelves with Poe
and Dickinson? Or was she herself afraid
to be swayed by the cooing doves, and live at odds
with the screaming hawks in her family?

The Latina maids are putting away the cups
and the silver spoons, sad to be missing out
on *música*—they seldom get to hear
in the hallowed halls. . . The valet sighs
as he rolls the carpets up and dusts the blinds.
Damn but a little Langston would be good
in this dreary mausoleum of a place!
Why does the White House have to be so white?
The chef from Baton Rouge is starved for verse
uncensored by Homeland Security.

NO POETRY UNTIL FURTHER NOTICE!
Instead the rooms are vacuumed and set up
for closed-door meetings planning an attack
against the ones who always bear the brunt
of silencing: the poor, the powerless,
those who must serve, those bearing poems, not arms.
So why be afraid of us, Mrs. Bush?
You're married to a scarier fellow.
We bring you tidings of great joy—
not only peace but poetry on earth.

Antler

56 YEARS OLD

MILWAUKEE, WISCONSIN

Antler is the author of Factory, Last Words *and* Antler: The Selected Poems. *He won the 1987 Witter Bynner Prize awarded annually "to an outstanding younger poet" by the American Academy and Institute of Arts and Letters in New York City, and the 1985 Walt Whitman Award, given by the Whitman Association of Camden, New Jersey to an author "whose contribution best reveals the continuing presence of Walt Whitman in American poetry." Of Antler's poetry, Allen Ginsberg said: "More fineness than I thought probable to see again in my lifetime from younger solitary unknown self-inspirer U.S. poet . . . one of Whitman's 'poets and orators to come.'"*

Draft-Dodgers vs. Poetry-Dodgers

Rather than fulfilling their military obligation,
   fulfilling their poetry obligation—
After all, what's more fulfilling,
   learning how to kill or love?
Those who become soldiers
   are evading the Poetry Service—
   dodging the Poetry Draft.
Isn't it their duty to their Country
   more to become a poet
   than a brainwashed murder robot?
When the young contemplate what branch
   of the Service to join,
They should know they can contemplate
   joining Poetry,
That Poetry is a Service that serves

the realization of Utopia
more than becoming skilled
at killing.
Too long it was thought the young were
needed to go to war,
Now the young are needed to go to peace.
Now the young are needed to go to poetry.

Electa Arenal (translator)

66 years old
New York

Translators: Electa Arenal is a translator of poetry and prose, and a specialist on Sor Juana Ines de la Cruz. Beatrix Gates has published three books of poetry, including In The Open, *a Lambda Literary Award finalist. Jesus Aguado, b. 1961 in Madrid, has lived in Seville and then Malaga since early childhood, and spent extended periods in Benares, India. He is the prize-winning author of eleven books of poetry and translated the work of Lawrence Ferlinghetti, among others.*

Untitled

Like the one who kills then skins a child,

grinds its bones,

         burns its tendons,

feeds the guts to a dog—

full of pride he calls a meeting

of parents, relatives and neighbors,

explains in unswerving detail

the minutiae of his cruel acts

and then requests that the community

puzzle the child back together again.

Vikram Babu asks:

are you like that?

from *Like the Oar That Cuts the Current: Poems of Vikram Babu* by Jesus Aguado; translated by Electa Arenal & Beatrix Gates

———

Elizabeth Austen

37 YEARS OLD
SEATTLE, WASHINGTON
Poet, teacher, gardener.

The Permanent Fragility of Meaning

Why persist, scratching across the white field,
row after row? Why repeat the ritual
every morning, emptying my hands,
asking for a new prayer to fold
and unfold?

      Nothing changes, no one is saved.

I walk into the day, hands still
empty, and beg
to be of use to someone. I lie down
in the dark and beg to believe
when the voice comes again with its commands,
with its promises—
      unfold your hands. Revelation
is not a fruit you pluck from trees. This is the work,
cultivating the smallest shoot, readying your tongue
to shape the sacred names, your mouth already filling—

I lie down in the dark.

I rise up and begin again.

Penelope Austin

52 YEARS OLD
ANN ARBOR, MICHAGAN/WILLIAMSPORT, PENNSYLVANIA
Disabled by breast cancer, I currently live in Ann Arbor to receive final treatment. My poems (all antiwar in some way) have appeared in Orion, APR, Kenyon Review, *and are forthcoming in the* Journal *and* The Tampa Review. *A collection,* Waiting For a Hero, *was published in 1988.*

War Breaks Out Again

All this way up the mountain and after all
all there is is a color, steel, maybe,
or jade, the color of a handcarved ring I carried
when I began to travel. A woman riding
the bus to Batu Feringhi told me jade
would save my life, and I believed her the day

in 1974 when I stooped to collect
the pieces of that ring that snapped as I
walked between two rows of Arab teenagers
levelling machine guns at my heart. I thought
I'd never travel again. But here I am,
still hiking upward. What have I learned of happiness?

Perhaps it would have been better to stop
halfway, looking over the valley sliced
into the Wasatch, autumn colors a comfort.
I stood fast as a bank of clouds rushed in
from the valley, coming at me until first the valley
disappeared, then the farther peaks,

the nearer, the canyon, all obliterated.
It was like going blind to the mountains, to the autumn,
blind to the cold, blind to the pungent red
pine, and blind to fear's trace in the mouth,
so the body no longer exists, not as a shadow,
a ghost, or a lost friend. Jade can't protect

us all. Still, I keep hiking as if I believe
in jade, which may be all that matters, for
beyond the new bank of clouds rolling
in from the west are walled fortresses, cities
of jade, of emerald, of stone, water, sky
the color of steel—I may as well believe.

———

Christopher Bakken

35 YEARS OLD
MEADVILLE, PENNSYLVANIA

Christopher Bakken's first book of poetry, After Greece, *was awarded the T. S. Eliot Prize in Poetry for 2001. He teaches at Allegheny College in Meadville, Pennsylvania.*

Ohio Elegy

I drive too fast with Cleveland
behind me, past stadiums and thirteen zip codes,
through rigid and red-blooded suburbs at dusk.
And instead of drinking
in the highway, its light-scattering steeples

and that mass of starlings released
like an unclenched fist from a line of hedges
I can't see, I'm thinking again of my country:
gray factories snoring outside Painesville
and the meat-packing plants of Ashtabula
—the one sow I imagine there,
scratching her bristled ass along that last steel chute
like the torturer's horse in Auden,
penned up in my mind tonight
with a hundred other agonies,
not the very least of them
redeeming us for war.

I speak too plainly here.
Such honesty betrays my desire to suffer silence
silently. I think of all the men
scuffling, somewhere, into concrete bunkers.
I think of Whitman patching the pulped arms of soldiers;
of James Wright humming Vallejo in Martin's Ferry.
I think of something that makes me resent the passage of time,
or the plain sense of passing here:
the greasy shanks of warehouse loading docks,
and haloed wrecks in truck stop lots,
and rabbits darting deeper into night.
I'm steering my way out of this day.
The fields of Ohio are giving up too,
slumped fences and stubble now briefly lit
when a phalanx of Hell's Angels
ratchets down the left lane,
busting up the monotony
of a landscape already
exhausted from waiting so long to wail.

John Balaban

John Balaban was the recipient of the 1998 William Carlos Williams Award and has been nominated for the National Book Award.

Collateral Damage

for Miss Tin in Hue

"The girl (captured; later, freed)
and I (collapsed by a snip of lead)
remember well the tea you steeped
for us in the garden, as music played
and the moon plied the harvest dusk.
You read the poem on a Chinese vase
that stood outside your father's room,
where he dozed in a mandarin dream
of King Gia Long's reposing at Ben Ngu.
We worry that you all are safe.
A house with pillars carved in poems
is floored with green rice fields
and roofed by all the heavens of this world."

. . . . . Well, that was the poem, written
in fullest discovery and iambics
by a twenty-four-year old feeling lucky
not long after those scary events.
Three years later, he (i.e. yours truly)
went back with his young American wife
(not the girl above "captured . . . freed, etc.")
and the night before the '72 Spring Offensive
(which, you'll recall, almost took the city)
tried to find Miss Tin's house once again
. . . . . in a thunderstorm, both wearing ponchos,

and he (a version of "me") clutching a .45 Colt
while she, just clutched his wet hand. Of course,
anyone might have shot us—the Viet Cong
infiltrating the city, the last Marines,
the jittery ARVN troops, or, really,
any wretch just trying to feed his family.
So here's the point: why would anyone
(esp. A: me, or B: my wife, or versions of same)
even dream of going out like that? . . . Simple:
A. To show his bride a household built on poems.
B. To follow love on all his lunkhead ventures.
Anyway, when we found the gated compound,
we scared the wits out of the Vietnamese inside
on the verandah reading by tiny kerosene lamps
or snoozing in hammocks under mosquito netting
who took us for assassins, or ghosts, until
my wife pulled off her poncho hood, revealing
the completely unexpected: a pretty. blonde. White Devil.
Since Miss Tin wasn't there, they did the right thing
and denied knowing her, as night and river
hissed with rain and a lone goose honked forlornly.

The next night, we headed out again,
the monsoon flooding the darkened city,
the offensive booming in nearby hills,
and montagnards trekking into Hue in single file
as their jungle hamlets fell to the barrage.
I kept our jeep running, as my wife dashed out
to give away our piasters to the poor
bastards half-naked in the driving rain.
She gave it all away. Six months' salary,
a sack of banknotes watermarked with dragons,

(except what we needed to get back to Saigon,
but that's another story) . . . the point here being:
I often think of Miss Tin's pillared house in Hue
and those events now thirty years ago
whenever leaders cheer the new world order,
or generals regret "collateral damage."

———

Tia Ballantine
HONOLULU, HAWAII

DESTINY IS MEMORY

After bombs remove oil-stained pavement, bricks,

and what's left of the garden wall, I find

a shoelace and three plastic cups designed

to look like Mickey Mouse. Under thick black

ash, a patch of blue. In for the long haul—

he'd say, shoulder pressed to mine, hands resting

on my thigh, breath collapsed. We'd watch western

skies go gray. Now, out of clouds, books fall:

Complete Milton lands near The Silent Clowns

Shakespeare breaks its spine against the carcass

of the kitchen sink. Pages flutter past

flame . . . kin with ken and kind with kind confound

disorder, horror, fear, and mutiny.

A fire burns the last remaining tree.

———

Willis Barnstone
Willis Barnstone was Pulitzer Prize finalist in poetry.

Waiting for the Barbarians

> *And now what will we do without the Barbarians?*
> —C. P. Cavafy

The emperor has no brains. His ministers, mentors
and minions know the condition of our leader
and administrate his mind with blatant tact,
and no one, not even his cowed opponents, breaks
the hypocritical code. The aura of silence about
the emperor's mind is mandated by expediency.
No child calls out: The emperor has no brains!

And we seem lost. Maybe the word hypocrisy
is severe to type a man who stumbled to his throne
on an orange, and fear makes him popular.
As regional crown prince he broke a record
for executing hooligans, each time blessing God
for his harsh mercy. The popular fears stays on.
We're united. Would you be profiled a traitor?

The emperor depends on the holy barbarians
who march in multitudes, who tremble the streets
down to their tar intestines. These ancient furies
tear their hair out and rip bras and blouses
from their bodies. Our leader prays softly at barbaric
hoots. They cry *Idiot!* They shriek *Face of Satan!*
Our monarch is pleased their wicked ways are loud.

Our people love a dumb emperor. He's one of us,
a common man with vices who likes a pistol,
a guy talking back to barbarians. He will bomb them
before they smash us. He smiles and looks frightened
yet it's sweet to be an emperor and host premiers,
athletes and heroes, and not live in a sewer
but in a great white house circled by big cannons.

There is melancholy in our land. And bad news.
Russians claim barbarians live only in the Caucuses
or have facelifts and own slot-machine parlors.
Are there no wild beasts in a desert once Eden?
Our emperor's men have gone underground
in panic but send up blueprints to create
a goat-horned dragon roaring over the ocean.

Our mindless caesar lies on the ground and weeps.
It is sad to live under a subnormal emperor.
We are tanking and he bumps along in his golfcart.
The barbarians were a solution. Another winter.
What can we do? We're obedient as Mongol ponies.
The emperor's minions haunt an underground city,
run secret courts and e-mail God for our next step.

We are waiting for the barbarians. Our emperor
has memorized his speech. He has no brains
yet our daughter comes home from school, saying:
Our emporer seems crudely smart and wicked.
Maybe our barbarian will not blow up the world
or fling us all in prison. The sad one smiles.
There is a terrible melancholy in our land.

Wendy Battin

Mondrian's Forest

> *in memory of Greg Levey,*
> *d. February 18, 1991*

1. February 19, 1991

Every car drones a radio,
every shop keeps the TV on.

The smart bombs are thinking their way
into Baghdad, on video grids, in primary colors,

and yesterday in the middle of Amherst, a man
drenched himself in gasoline and lit a match.

Next to the body bagged on the Commons,
"Peace" on a sheet of cardboard, and his

driver's license, safe, and the old oaks
safe, only the grass charred.

Already the papers have found
neighbors willing to say that he'd *seemed depressed*,

someone to call him *isolated*.
Nine Cambodian Buddhists come

down from Leverett in their saffron robes
to pray. Two Veterans of Foreign Wars

heckle over the chants and the slow
gong, a circle of voices on the block of lawn.

2. Trees on the Gein, With Rising Moon (1908)

When Mondrian began
his world held rivers and trees, but not

the water's compliance and not
the ash's stillness, for he was in them.

He stood five trees against a red sky;
floated five more

in the mirror of the red river,
all ten wringing their black trunks

into green.
The trees on the water are breaking up,

breaking up, and still remain
trees in the center of their dissolution.

The trees on the bank flame up inside
their heavy outlines:

imagine a death in a man that pushes
first here then there at the lively

pliable skin. The limbs
distend, too full of ripening.

Thick oils eddy and ripple, a slick
on the turbulence of things.

3. Bodhi

Today on the woods trail by Amethyst Brook,
I prayed, *Kuan Yin*. Kuan Yin, enthroned

in the Asian Museum, enormous in limestone.
"She who hears the cries of the world,"

her spine sheer as a bluff, and both hands open.
I couldn't say if the polished eyes

were open or lidded. *In the new representation,*
reason takes first place, wrote Mondrian,

his labor then to save the trees from the wind,
to rescue his clean strict sight from the eyes

in his head, that saw only through blood.
I'm not one for praying, but somehow the ice

breaking up, the meltwater surge
of the brook gouged her name from my throat,

the way it gouges the bank out from under the trees
and digs bare the root-weave. Not she

who answers the cries, Kuan Yin. Not she who consoles.
Her body is still, is stone:

She who will not kindle and blaze
when she hears a man burn.

Marvin Bell

65 years old
Iowa City, Iowa
Professor, University of Iowa. Poet Laureate, State of Iowa. Veteran, U.S. Army. Independent voter.

A Lesson from the Corps

When you find the body, it has cauliflower ears.
It stinks of dead worms, the blood crumbles
        between your fingers.
When you find the body, the sleeves of the combat
        fatigues are in shreds.
Its face is puce, its torso black and blue, its
        guts purple, but the teeth still gleam, and
        the bones will shine up when cleaned.
Your saliva congeals, you taste dried paste.
Later, you may feel shame for noticing the colors
        or hating the smell.
You were schooled to do this.
To yank the dog tag off with a snap.
You were trained not to answer back to the
        silence.
There is a hiss as you compel the metal tag
        between the teeth.

This day may become a whiteout, a glare, a deficit
        in memory.
A place too barren even for a shriek.
A picture that didn't develop, just a clear
        negative.
For nothing recorded the thump of the bullet as it

hit, nor the webbing wet inside his helmet
liner, nor the echoing within the helmet
itself.
But you may think you remember the shudder you
didn't see when he died.
You may imagine the last word, the mouth before
the lingering stare.
The machinery of his broken chest may appear in
dreams.
You may see the eyes, and hear the last expulsion
of air.
He is the vault now for your questions to God.
Only the dead can tell you the distance from here
to there.

———

James Bertolino

THE NEW RAPTURE

The saved will be those
whose bodies
are vaporized,
whose lives rise toward heaven
in the bomb-clouds.

The damned will be those
who survive.

Sarah Blackman

22 YEARS OLD
LOS ANGELES, CALIFORNIA/SEOUL, SOUTH KOREA
I am currently in between stints of being a student. Living in Los Angeles. Visiting friends in South Korea, where antiwar sentiment has almost seamlessly become anti-American sentiment in tandem with our increasing military presence.

Syria, 1997

At dawn the salt flats
are the backbone of a country.
A man is taking his sheep to market,
another is spitting in the streets.

Moving from sleep to grey
light I am always in the desert.
Now, the streets flood. Gutters
clog with dirty ice, pine needles,
oil roses climbing the trellis
of coffee cups and plastic spoons.

What cities. What deserts,
mountains, rivers, steaming
sewers, marble towers struck by air.

What wars, buckled concrete,
burned kiosks, rubble,
silence, lidless sleep.

What men waking in darkness,
taking the sheep to market,

laughing at their own voice,
walking down long roads,
turning, going home.

———

Helen Blackshear
91 YEARS OLD
MONTGOMERY, ALABAMA
Teacher, National Pen Women awards, books, poems, chapbooks, many awards, Alabama poet laureate (eighth) 1995–1999

Search and Destroy

"I thought how it must have been
        for you in World War two,"
                Jimmy wrote his dad.
"I figured if you could take it,
        I could too."

He wrote again after his pals were killed.
(With football triumphs
        ringing in their ears,
                they'd egged each other on
                        to join the Green Berets.
Now two of them were gone
        in nameless valleys
                where there were no cheers.)

"I've made a brand new friend,

      this huge black guy
           who seems to feel I'm just a kid.
He sticks around and tries to shield
      me from doing drugs and stuff.
Yesterday he kept me from getting killed."

The letters stopped.
      That was the last we heard
           until finally we had official word:
"On a search and destroy mission,
      he failed to return."
           And that was all.

Now he remains as a name
      on a long black wall.

Robert Bly

Robert Bly is a poet, translator and fiction writer. Light Around the Body *won the National Book Award.*

Call and Answer

Tell me why it is we don't lift our voices these days
And cry over what is happening. Have you noticed
The plans are made for Iraq and the ice cap is melting?

I say to myself: "Go on, cry. What's the sense
Of being an adult and having no voice? Cry out!
See who will answer! This is Call and Answer!"

We will have to call especially loud to reach
Our angels, who are hard of hearing; they are hiding
In the jugs of silence filled during our wars.

Have we agreed to so many wars that we can't
Escape from silence? If we don't lift our voices, we allow
Others (who are ourselves) to rob the house.

How come we've listened to the great criers—Neruda,
Akhmatova, Thoreau, Frederick Douglass—and now
We're silent as sparrows in the little bushes?

Some masters say our life lasts only seven days.
Where are we in the week? Is it Thursday yet?
Hurry, cry now! Soon Sunday night will come.

———

George Bowering
Vancouver, British Columbia, Canada
Poet Laureate of Canada

Statement of Conscience

Someone, please introduce the idea of God, if not Christianity, into the Cabinet of the USA, and tell these eerie people that killing children is wrong, that the U.S. becomes every day more and more frightful. Is this what the daily Pledge of Allegiance in elementary schools leads to? Please do not use your weapons of mass destruction on my world, Americans!

Geoff Brock

Poetry & the American Voice

> *after the symposium of the same name,*
> *arranged by Laura Bush in the shadow*
> *of war, then cancelled out of fear*
> *that it would be "politicized"*

My day was spent struggling to write
the wrong poem. Now it's night,
and I can't sleep—
so many shepherds have turned to sheep,

and that kind can't be counted on.
In London and in Washington
they stand together
(Ms. Bush chats poetry or weather)

on roads that lead to a slaughterhouse.
And if there comes a dissenting voice,
a cautious word
whispered or shouted, it isn't heard.

Along our country's eastern coast,
the Bush league plans its war. They boast
of "an attack
that will unleash upon Iraq

levels of force that have never been
imagined before, much less seen"—

as if this were
something desirable in a war.

Across the ocean, Blair abets.
He may be just one of Bush's pets,
but blood will be
on his hands too. "Democracy,"

like "Jesus," is a word men use
when it's convenient, an excuse
for having no
excuse. And those who ought to know

its meaning don't. The media class
renounce analysis en masse.
Even the pen
that co-wrote "All the President's Men"

now scribbles only the party line;
if his first book was a gold mine,
then "Bush at War"
is just the shaft. It's a thick bore,

an emblem, sad as a requiem,
for what our press has now become.
Meanwhile Ms. Bush
invites some poets for a posh

symposium on Dickinson
and Whitman and Hughes, as if they'd gone
Bob Woodward's way.
But what would those three feel today?

They'd have, like me, the weary blues.
Does anybody think that Hughes
(harassed then by
McCarthy and the FBI)

would have attended if living now?
Or Whitman, who knew exactly how
the oval office,
beneath its democratic surface,

was "bought and sold and prostituted"?
Or Dickinson? She might have recited
"It feels a shame
to be Alive—." Or mailed it, framed.

Laura Bush's American Voice
contains no multitudes. The choice
she offers: sing
in chorus with our unelected king

or hush. "Come sing," she says, "with me.
We'll dip some hummus, nibble brie . . ."
while "shock and awe"
reign there—and here—in lieu of law.

Colleen Morton Busch

33 YEARS OLD
BERKELEY, CANADA
Colleen Morton Busch is an editor at Yoga Journal *magazine.*

Belief

They don't want to go
anywhere, they say they only want peace,
women who sift mortar

through thinned fingers like flour.
The only sun: the cellar's fire
beating bread into bricks.

I hardly knew you
three women, sitting with Médoc
and bread between your knees.

The one with cropped brown hair
that fell to the side and followed
the smooth slope of the brow,

told me about your country
in a voice soft like milk going down,
firming the bones from inside.

You leaned into one another
with the purpose of flowers
folding out of a clear vase, your legs,

stems curled around glass edges
and swept to the side, your fingers,
petals pale as water.

My loved and forgotten faces,
gunfire blasts the hospital
and workers lift a body from the ground.

Your country's in the news.
Your men lift their guns, lift each other
into trucks big enough for the dead,

and your arms must rise
above a lover who bleeds,
looks at your face the last time and believes
your bare skin on the green grass could save him.

———

Hayden Carruth
Hayden Carruth has been awarded the National Book Critic's Circle Award and the National Book Award.

COMPLAINT AND PETITION

Mr. President: On a clear cold
morning I address you from a remote
margin of your dominion in plain-
style Yankee quatrains because

I don't know your exalted language
of power. I'm thankful for that. This
is a complaint and petition, sent
to you in the long-held right I claim

as a citizen. To recapitulate your
wrong-doings is unnecessary; the topic
is large and prominent and already
occupies the attention of historians

and political scholars, whose findings
will in the near future expose your
incontinent and maniacal ambition
for all to see. Let it suffice to

say that you have warped the law and
flouted the will and wisdom of the
people as no other has before you.
You have behaved precisely as a tin-pot

tyrant in any benighted, inglorious
corner of the earth. And now you are
deviously and corruptly manipulating
events in order to create war.

Let us speak plainly. You wish to
murder millions, as you yourself
have said, to appease your fury. We
oppose such an agenda—we, the people,

artists, artisans, builders, makers,
honest American men and women,
especially the poets, for whom I dare
to speak. We say, desist, resign,

hide yourself in your own shame,
lest otherwise the evil you have
loosed will destroy everything
and love will quit the world.

Tom Chandler
RHODE ISLAND
Tom Chandler is the poet laureate of Rhode Island.

The War

The sand and crumbled rock
pocked with caves, scorched
craters, the boy with one eye
tending a goat, the old woman's
leather face, age forty-two
the caption reads, the city
with walls the color of sunshine,
the bloody crowd screaming
curses at the naked body
twisting like a piece of meat
on a pole, the tiny newspaper
map, the place names carved
of hard consonants, the arc
of black arrows pointing
fingers at the whole idea.

Patricia Clark

Grand Rapids, Michigan
I am the author of North of Wondering *(poems, 1999). Other poems have appeared recently in* Atlantic Monthly, Poetry, *and* Slate.

Riverside Ghazal

Most watery of all the trees, these willows
stand in water. Ice pools around the ankles of willows.

A tree's name should reveal its nature.
Salix babylonica: the first word is for willow.

Doesn't it sound stretchy and pliable?
Babylonica is for the weeping part of willow.

From a quotation in Psalms: by the rivers of Babylon
we wept. The people hung harps on willows.

The weight gave them a bent, permanent shape.
A girl flings her hair down, a young willow.

A golden color, like a shout, all the length
of the fronds. They light up the willow.

Nearby on the concrete ramp, an ice-filled boat
waits for the sun to unmoor it, sail it past the willows.

In the season of thaw, this ice giving way.
By the rivers of America, we wept these willows.

Lucille Clifton

stones and bones

here is a country where old men
gather in the capital and
speak their language filled with
stones
their syllables are chips of bone
they speak of lifting up a creed
while cold and still there under
their tongue is somebody else's child
or mine
bones and stones
our ears bleed
red and white and blue

Alfred Corn
60 YEARS OLD
OKLAHOMA
Author of nine books of poems, the most recent, Contradictions.

LETTER TO SAM HAMILL

(After Sam Hamill's call for poems protesting Laura Bush's
invitation to a Symposium on American Poetry at the White
House)

Sam, I keep thinking it's not really fitting
To send a "no thanks" when I wasn't invited.

And I'm glad I won't have to be cold to a person
Apparently decent and kind, a reader
Whose outlook poems and fictions have broadened.

Loyal, I think, to this nation, I hereby
Inculpate myself for making slapdash,
Insufficient and tardy efforts to save it
From the brutal, disastrous, avoidable brink
Our misguided Executive and Congress have brought us to.
Demonstrations, petitions, and reasoning seldom
Make an impression on heat-packing chauvinists,
They don't give a flying . . . whatever, bent as they
Are on showing the world who's in charge.

The practice of politics (always beyond belief
Boring) will take care of *us* if we fail
To take care of *it*. Despair is suburban,
So we soldier on, casting our ballots for candidates
Who won't be elected, we write those who were,
We canvass and organize. No, in all honesty
I can't, at age sixty, pretend I would welcome
Being clubbed or imprisoned; but I do root for those
Nonviolent actions performed in the interest
Of liberty, justice, and peace—for Americans,
Sure, but as well for all people everywhere.
To save the skin of one Arab, Israeli, or Yank
Would I write an obvious poem? You bet I would!
If only it could save. When gauging results
Of our deeds, though, I take an agnostic approach.
Seek justice: The aftermath's not in our hands.
Since "All wars are boyish," would that all war
Criminals present and future would grow up
And not dream it's cool or effective to pistolwhip
Erstwhile allies they've turned into enemies.

Should one ever resort to violent measures
In the name of a righteous cause? I'd say not.
Aren't we a global concern, the Blue Planet's
Symbiotic affiliates? Yes, because no man
Or nation's an island, entire of itself.
If the bell should toll for Iraq or for Palestine,
It will toll for these States and Israel, too—
For the threatened ideals of fair play and loveliness
Embodied in poems we're moved to live by.

PFC Corn here, reporting for peace watch.

Peter Coyote

Flags

Flags are everywhere.
Tied to cars, strapped
to twisted girders, fanning the air
where silver needles have pierced
the steel ribs of a bold idea,
tossing hope to the teeth of gravity
cinching the collar on a world
straining to breathe.
Men are lifting broken children
from stones in Beirut. A flop-eared mutt
guards a human foot in Bosnia.
Stacked skulls peek

through lianas in Cambodia, while a fireman
breathes into the mouth
of a dead infant in Oklahoma.
The cookies of mothers, pomegranates, musky sheets
of marriage beds, pistachios and birthday cakes
are drenched in oily smoke and iron slag. Everywhere,
electrons serve only their own will,
heavy metals float as ash. Gaps appear
in every skyline. Everywhere, flags
open their wings in the hearts
of people, flutter in the corner of my tv
while a man who thinks he is speaking,
barks, his lips
slick with marrow.

The prep-school boys
are rampaging again. The palm-frond bars
stocking brewskis, and 'gimme'-hats
for the dead-drop boys,
the dirty secret boys,
from El Mozote and Panama,
off to Baghdad and Kabul now,
dropping in to Peshawar.—
Their itineraries clot the tongue
blood leaks from the ears of history.
The Class of '55 boys
are crazy for bottle-neck flies.
Soot-stained
snapshots, an upturned chair, a thumb—
—everywhere people are weeping and afraid,
waving flags, plotting check and mate,
as if one smooth move might rid the world

of shadows. They are burying
Jews in Tel Aviv, lofting flag-wrapped martyrs
in Ramallah, cursing the mourners in New York.
Everywhere, there is emptiness, tattered space
where someone once sauntered
or warmed their hands with steaming chestnuts.
Each banner a thousand deaths
somewhere
each flag a sword, or swooning plane,
somewhere,
each snapping pennant taps
a riddle in code:
can the heart of a people
be opened by a killer?
Closed by a leader?
Numbed to suffering even
as it weeps?

The dead
in Chile are poems,
in Nicaragua palms and vines;
in Yugoslavia catalogued in Brussels,
in Baghdad irradiated dirt.
In New York, dust
drifting on sills
and dashboards through vaporized glass,
dancing in freshets of air that whisper,
startling those holding their breaths
to hear the faintest of cries.
And the hard man with the soft eyes
resting in the shadows of poppies,
negotiates with the lavender angel

the number of souls required
as threads in a flag
woven to the glory
for Allah.

Autumn Equinox, 2001.

———

Reba Crawford-Hayes

11 YEARS OLD

OAKLAND, CALIFORNIA

I am an eleven-year-old girl and I am in the sixth grade. Most of the kids in my school don't want a war with Iraq. We wish that President Bush would stop being the school yard bully and do what Jesus would do—fight evil with good, not evil with evil. It says it right in the Bible.

WAR

Wet bodies of those who have fallen
Afghanistan blown to pieces!
Right on target—the men, the women,
the children, crying mommy, mommy!

———

Robert Creeley
BUFFALO, NEW YORK

Ground Zero

What's after or before
seems a dull locus now
as if there ever could be more

or less of what there is,
a life lived just because
it is a life if nothing more.

The street goes by the door
just like it did before.
Years after I am dead,

there will be someone here instead
perhaps to open it,
look out to see what's there—

even if nothing is,
or ever was,
or somehow all got lost.

Persist, go on, believe.
Dreams may be all we have,
whatever one believe

of worlds wherever they are—
with people waiting there
will know us when we come

when all the strife is over,
all the sad battles lost or won,
all turned to dust.

Alfred de Zayas

55 YEARS OLD
GENEVA, SWITZERLAND

J.D., Harvard, 1970, D.Ph., Göttingen, 1977; member, New York Bar; visiting professor of international law at various universities; Secretary of P.E.N. Centre of the Suisse Romande (French-speaking Switzerland); former Secretary of the United Nations Human Rights committee; retired early from the UN in 2003 in order to devote more time to teaching, writing, research.

Beatitudes

Can you tell me who is good and who is bad?
The ancient "we and they" divides us artificially.
Yet for the children of New York and Baghdad
only one equation counts: their shared humanity.

Woe upon the men who would unleash a war
regardless of the risks, impervious to the law!
Alas, the many nations that such crimes abhor
may fail to stop the programmed "Shock and Awe".

But silence now would make us guilty too.
Protest we must: Prevent "preventive war"!

Who are the victims, who the victimizers? Who?
Ourselves, our leaders! To the White House: Mirror!

Blest are the peacemakers, children of our God.* Deplore
the wielders of the sword: they must one day account.
Now George is seen in church, but does he grasp the core
of Christianity? The Sermon on the Mount.

*Matthew 5:9

Mark Doty

*Mark Doty has been awarded the National Book Critic's Circle Award
and the T. S. Eliot Prize.*

Statement of Conscience

Poetry has always been a voice for those without voices, a
cry and a song lifted up in service of humanity, in praise of
life, in lament for lives lost, in hope for the future. Those
values—praise of life, hope for the future—are, sadly, anti-
thetical to the policies this administration is practicing
abroad. The human consequences of an unnecessary war
will be unspeakable. We've already seen the consequences
of this administration's indifference to the environment
and to the poor, its disinterest in the rights of women, of
racial and sexual minorities. I am proud that American
poets are speaking back to the White House. Our art
attempts to serve what is best in people, and it requires of

us that we stand up and say a firm "No" to war-making, to profiteering, to the careless destruction of life.

———

Rita Dove
Rita Dove was the U.S. poet laureate from 1993 to 1995.

UMOJA: EACH ONE OF US COUNTS

One went the way of water,
one crumpled under stone;
one climbed the air but plunged through fire,
one fought the fear alone.

Remember us, though we are gone.

A star flares on an epaulet,
a ball rolls in harm's way;
the glowing line onscreen goes flat,
an anonymous bullet strays—

Remember us! Do not forget!

One lay slathered in garlands,
one left only a smear;
one cracked a joke, smiled, then shrugged
to show he didn't care.

Do not forget that we were here.

Do those who failed still miss the wind,
that sweet breath from the sky?
Do they still covet rock and moss
or the swift, hard blink of the lizard's eye?

We walk on water, we are written on air.

Let us honor the lost, the snatched, the
relinquished,
those vanquished by glory, muted by shame.
Stand up in the silence they've left and listen:
those absent ones, unknown and unnamed—

remember!

their whispers fill the arena.

Len Edgerly

52 YEARS OLD
DENVER
*A recent graduate of the Bennington Writing Seminars MFA program,
I have published poetry in* The Beloit Poetry Journal, New York
Quarterly, *and* High Plains Literary Review.

*DOING ZAZEN ON THE SNOW
IN FRONT OF THE COLORADO STATE CAPITOL
AN UNKNOWN NUMBER OF DAYS
BEFORE MY COUNTRY ATTACKS IRAQ*

I'm new at this,
unsure of my arguments.

Iraq is one of the world's largest producers of dates.

I should have worn wool socks.

Last week a friend offered me a white button.
I said, "I'm against war, but not ready to wear a button."

Time's up.

I fold my plastic sheet.
My body's melted a hole in the snow
where my legs used to be.

A man in mittens hands me a button.

I'm wearing it now,
        ready to be written down.

Lynnell Edwards

38 YEARS OLD
PORTLAND, OREGON
I am associate professor of English at Concordia University in Portland, Oregon where I teach a variety of writing and literature classes. My first volume of poetry is forthcoming from Red Hen Press in June 2003.

The Weather in Herat

In the west again it will be sunny,
a hot brillance, air sharp as the jagged peaks
scowling down the dry basin, visibility
clear to the border where the horizon
warps into planes of heat.

These are things we can know,
intelligible signs of temperature,
cloud cover, visibility, fog.

Our icons are precise, one cold
note sounding over
the wailing incantations of sorrow.

Ours is a hard geometry yoked against
the dizzy pattern of fringe and color.

But when the blue sky cracks and the dust explodes
and a figure hard and insect old,
rises, impenetrable as bone, to crawl
across the aching earth, then we too will
know the places with names like hills:
Jalalabad, Herat, Kandahar, Kabul,
clattering like teeth, bared behind the veil.

Sebastian Eggert

50 years old
Port Townsend, Washington
I'm a woodworker. I provide family wage jobs for working-class people and try to live an honest and quiet life supporting my family, friends, and community.

Compression

In a darkened corner of the shop
      the old compressor chugs its steady beat.
The metronomic rhythm the sound of
      growing pressure.

The same beat we hear
      in the air of this heated debate.
That relentless pounding
      of what seems to be our country's march to war.

We marched against a war, long ago,
      wondering if it would make a difference.
Now we march again, in conscience, knowing.
      We cannot allow this lie to go unchallenged.

The motor off now,
      The piston silent.
It will let off pressure slowly, then cycle on again.
      I often wonder when that old metal tank will blow.

Martín Espada

45 years old, Amherst, Massachusetts
Martín Espada is the author of seven poetry collections, including Alabanza: New and Selected Poems, 1982-2002.

Alabanza: In Praise of Local 100

> *For the 43 members of Hotel Employees and Restaurant Employees Local 100, working at the Windows on the World restaurant, who lost their lives in the attack on the World Trade Center*

Alabanza. Praise the cook with a shaven head
and a tattoo on his shoulder that said *Oye,*
a blue-eyed Puerto Rican with people from Fajardo,
the harbor of pirates centuries ago.
Praise the lighthouse in Fajardo, candle
glimmering white to worship the dark saint of the sea.
Alabanza. Praise the cook's yellow Pirates cap
worn in the name of Roberto Clemente, his plane
that flamed into the ocean loaded with cans for Nicaragua,
for all the mouths chewing the ash of earthquakes.
Alabanza. Praise the kitchen radio, dial clicked
even before the dial on the oven, so that music and Spanish
rose before bread. Praise the bread. *Alabanza.*

Praise Manhattan from a hundred and seven flights up,
like Atlantis glimpsed through the windows of an ancient
  aquarium.
Praise the great windows where immigrants from the
  kitchen
could squint and almost see their world, hear the chant of
  nations:

Ecuador, México, Republica Dominicana,
Haiti, Yemen, Ghana, Bangladesh.
Alabanza. Praise the kitchen in the morning,
where the gas burned blue on every stove
and exhaust fans fired their diminutive propellers,
hands cracked eggs with quick thumbs
or sliced open cartons to build an altar of cans.
Alabanza. Praise the busboy's music, the *chime-chime*
of his dishes and silverware in the tub.
Alabanza. Praise the dish-dog, the dishwasher
who worked that morning because another dishwasher
could not stop coughing, or because he needed overtime
to pile the sacks of rice and beans for a family
floating away on some Caribbean island plagued by frogs.
Alabanza. Praise the waitress who heard the radio in the
   kitchen
and sang to herself about a man gone. *Alabanza.*

After the thunder wilder than thunder,
after the shudder deep in the glass of the great windows,
after the radio stopped singing like a tree full of terrified frogs,
after night burst the dam of day and flooded the kitchen,
for a time the stoves glowed in darkness like the lighthouse
   in Fajardo,
like a cook's soul. Soul I say, even if the dead cannot tell us
about the bristles of God's beard because God has no face,
soul I say, to name the smoke-beings flung in constellations
across the night sky of this city and cities to come.
Alabanza I say, even if God has no face.

Alabanza. When the war began, from Manhattan and Kabul
two constellations of smoke rose and drifted to each other,
mingling in icy air, and one said with an Afghan tongue:

Teach me to dance. We have no music here.
And the other said with a Spanish tongue:
I will teach you. Music is all we have.

Sascha Feinstein
39 YEARS OLD
WILLIAMSPORT, PENNSYLVANIA
Sascha Feinstein won the Hayden Carruth Award for his poetry collection, Misterioso. *He teaches at Lycoming College and edits the journal* Brilliant Corners.

Blue Herons

Against a window of unresolved
   Morning light, the martini's
      Triangle floats a lemon rind
Like a goldfish. Again, she's risen

Before five, muscles in her back
   Contracting for heat.
      "The cost," she'll tell me,
"Of wedging stoneware."

Tossed by someone never seen,
   The Herald hits her door with news
      She's avoiding—ground war—
So for now she leaves the paper

Tucked into itself, corks the merlot,
  Smooths the pillows—evidence
    Of her small divorce party.
From all-night wood firings,

Her body smells gray,
  "Seasoned," she likes to say,
    Smiling like her porcelain portraits:
Pre-Raphaelite lips, hair spiraling

Into grapevines and honeysuckle.
  On a milk pitcher: blue roses
    Within a matte ebony finish.
Touching those engraved petals,

I told her of a lagoon in the Yucatàn
  Where I held my breath to crawl
    Down a collage of basalt caverns,
How the walls pulsed and shimmered

As iridescent, indigo fish
  Emerged and withdrew
    Until I let go and rose,
Desperate as a flame for oxygen.

It's almost time
  To open the kiln, smoldering
    In the dawn's amber fog,
And her vision's spinning with possibility:

If the handful of rock salt
  Thrown in the ninth hour

Exploded perfectly
Into a nebula of glaze,

If the goblets kept their shape,
    If the soup tureen's heavy lid
        Still settles within its rim.
She unfolds her newspaper to face

Part of her broken world:
    Static-stricken charts
        Of missiles navigating
Baghdad at midnight

And clotted Gulf shores,
    Those nearly successful efforts
        To cleanse the feathers of
Blue herons paralyzed in oil.

———

Lawrence Ferlinghetti

Lawrence Ferlinghetti is San Francisco's first poet laureate (1998) and the owner and founder of City Lights Bookstore. This poem first appeared on the City Lights website (www.citylights.com).

Speak Out

And a vast paranoia sweeps across the land
And America turns the attack on its Twin Towers
Into the beginning of the Third World War
The war with the Third World

And the terrorists in Washington
Are shipping out the young men
To the killing fields again

And no one speaks

And they are rousting out
All the ones with turbans
And they are flushing out
All the strange immigrants

And they are shipping all the young men
To the killing fields again

And no one speaks

And when they come to round up
All the great writers and poets and painters
The National Endowment of the Arts of Complacency
Will not speak

While all the young men
Will be killing all the young men
In the killing fields again

So now is the time for you to speak
All you lovers of liberty
All you lovers of the pursuit of happiness
All you lovers and sleepers
Deep in your private dream
Now is the time for you to speak
O silent majority
Before they come for you!

Helen Frost

53 YEARS OLD
FORT WAYNE, INDIANA
Author of Keesha's House *and* Skin of a Fish, Bones of a Bird. *Website: www.helenfrost.com*

Shore

It has not happened yet. We
can move our minds together as
shorebirds rise above an ocean,
arc in evening light—grey silver white—
rise higher, turn, and find a way
together back to land.

January 2003

———

Tess Gallagher

I Have Never Wanted to March

or to wear an epaulet. Once I did
walk in a hometown parade to celebrate
a salmon derby. I was seven, my hair in
pigtails, and I wore a steel flasher strapped
diagonally across my chest like a bandolier
(which in Catalan would be bandolera from
bandoler meaning "bandit.") My black
bandit boots were rubber

because here on the flanks of the Olympics
it always rains on our parades.

I believe I pushed a doll buggy.
I believe all parades, especially military
parades could be improved if
the soldiers wore bandoliers made to attract
fish, and if each soldier pushed a doll buggy
inside which were real-seeming babies
with their all-seeing doll-eyes open
to reflect the flight of birds, of balloons
escaped from the hands of children to
hover over the town—higher than flags, higher
than minarets and steeples.

What soldier could forget about
collateral damage with those baby faces
locked to their chin straps? It is
conceivable that soldiers would resist
pushing doll buggies. Bending over
might spoil the rigidity of their marching.
What about a manual exhorting the patriotic
duty of pushing doll buggies? Treatises
on the symbolic meaning would need to be
written. Hollywood writers might be of use.
Poets and historians could collaborate,
reminding the marchers of chariots, of
Trojan horses, of rickshaws, of any wheeled
conveyance ever pulled or pushed or driven
in the service of human kind.

I would like, for instance, to appear
in the next parade as a Trojan horse. When

they open me I'll be seven years old.
There will be at least seven of me
inside me, for effect, and because it is
a mystical number. I won't understand
much about war, in any case—especially
its good reasons. I'll just want to be pushed
over some border into enemy territory, and
when no one's thinking anything except: what
a pretty horse! I'll throw open myself
like a flank and climb out, all
seven of me, like a many-legged spider
of myself. I'll speak only
in poetry, my second language, because it
is beautifully made for exploring the miraculous
ordinary event—in which an alchemy
of words agrees to apprentice itself to the possible
as it evades the impossible. Also poetry

doesn't pretend to know answers and speaks best
in questions, the way children do
who want to know everything, and don't believe
only what they're told. I'll be seven
unruly children when they open me up,
and I'll invite the children of the appointed enemy
to climb into my horse for a ride. We'll be secret
together, the way words are
the moment before they are spoken—
those Trojan horses of silence, looking for a border

to roll across like over-sized toys
manned by serious children—until one horse
has been pushed back and forth

with its contraband of mutually-pirated children
so many times that it is clear to any adult watching
this unseemly display, that enemy territory
is everywhere when anyone's child is at stake, when
the language of governments is reduced to ultimatums
and threats, when it wants to wear epaulets
and to march without
its doll buggy.

But maybe an edict or two could be made
by one child-ventriloquist through the mouth
of the horse, proposing that the advent of atrocities
be forestalled by much snorting, neighing, prancing and
tail swishing, by long, exhausted parades
of reciprocal child-hostages who may be
rescued only in the language of poetry
which insists on being lucid
and mysterious at once, like a child's hand
appearing from the peep-hole under the tail
of the horse, blindly waving to make sure that anyone
lined up along the street does not submit entirely
to the illusion of their absence, their
ever-squandered innocence, their hyper-responsive
minds in which a ladybug would actually fly away
with only its tiny flammable wings
to save its children from the burning house.

Martin Galvin

Army Burn Ward

First the doctor peels dead skin away.

"Debriding," like a teacher, names it.

(Like a virgin, like a pockmarked whore.)

Then the whirlpool, pain-pull spiralling down

like fire, like broken birds inside him.

(Like a winter wedded to the bone.)

Then the grafting, four long strips of skin.

"Rebriding," in his shock he giggles,

(Gagging like a schoolboy, like a groom.)

gagging as his new skin wrinkles, worms,

rejecting him. Again the whirlpool

(Like an April pain in soft swarms twirled.)

wheels and stops. The sink-plug pulled, he stares

(Like an empty coat, a burned-out star.)

unblinking as the brides inside him die.

Galen Garwood

At Wat Umong

Wat Umong lies close to the city,
Not far from the wrenching metal web of cars,
Motorcycles, tuks tuks, songthaous and
The black gas and oil that propels the world.
The noise, stink and debris
Of human violation end abruptly here.
In this quiet forest monastery,
There is no startling, golden Chedi to bring the buses
Of tourists.
No hawkers of banal artifacts. No
Balm for the misguided.

There is only the low rhythmic drone
Of chanting monks, and gentle light
Falls through dense canopies of green shadows and curls
Across ancient broken statues.
There are caves here,
Made centuries ago, dark
And full of smoke and incense
And the cool breath of the Buddha. The stone
Floor is polished by the bodies of prayers.

Nearby is a lotus-filled lake made ruddy
By the swirling appetite of fish.
For good luck, you can feed them,
And feed black swans if you wish or giant
Turtles that crawl into the sun. The sky
Above is clear but in the far West

Dark, bloody clouds press and coil
Against a rising moon.
I am told they come from men
Whose teeth have grown
Sharp as razors,
And whose hunger cannot be sated.

Chiangmai,
February 16, 2003.

———

Ted Genoways

30 YEARS OLD
IOWA CITY
Ted Genoways is the author of Bullroarer: A Sequence *and translator of* The Selected Poems of Miguel Hernandez. *He has also edited a new volume of the letters of Walt Whitman, forthcoming from Iowa, and edition of the worker-poet Joseph Kalar, forthcoming from Illinois.*

Rural Electric

—Bayard, Nebraska, June 1945

The workcrew worked closer, standing poles into postholes,
while the boy, not yet my father, watched at the window,

men sinking timbers, straight and tarred black as
exclamation points

that trailed banner headlines, set boldface in inky
   newsprint

as if to conquer the silence, but soon the night house
droned like a hive, tungsten-hum and the constant buzz

of the radio's blue tubes drowning out where he was
months later when programs were interrupted for the
   news

from Japan, leaving only dim memories: years lit by
   kerosene,
days at the window watching the workcrew working,

that last innocent night by the glow of the moon,
waiting for the second the blast and flash would fill the
   room.

Statement of Conscience

In July 1917, Siegfried Sassoon composed his famous
statement of conscientious objection "as an act of wilful
defiance of military authority, because I believe that the
war is being deliberately prolonged by those who have the
power to end it." Here now, we stand at a still more dan-
gerous precipice, because I believe that war is being perpe-
trated by those who have the power to avoid it. As poets,
we are obligated to speak out against this prospect, even as
it begins to appear an eventuality. Disgusted as I am by the
reprehensible actions of our unelected leaders, I am
equally appalled by the ignorance displayed by Laura Bush

when she states that "it would be inappropriate to turn a literary event into a political forum." No doubt she would have found it inappropriate for Walt Whitman to speak out against the horrors of the Civil War or Wilfred Owen to decry the use of mustard gas in World War I or Miguel Hernandez to warn of coming floods of blood if no one opposed the Fascists in Spain. Certainly the First Lady would not have supported the conscientious objection of William Stafford during World War II or Faiz Ahmed Faiz's questions about the purges during the partition of India or Robert Bly's open opposition to Vietnam. She is wrong, as this entire administration is wrong. A literary event is an ideal political forum, and we must not fail the generations of poets who came before us by falling silent now.

———

John Gery

Spring Offensive

> *So little cause for carolings . . .*
> —Thomas Hardy

The birds keep singing in the dark
as undeterred as Englishmen
in Africa; my neighbors quiet—
sound asleep—I lie here stark
and fast, near the millennium,

bewildered and as unconsoled
by all the things I thought I knew
as empires by their allies.—Still,
this music fills my room, unspoiled
as though it were the one thing true
my country hasn't tried to kill

or bind into its vast regime.
If I, too, could only sing, instead
of tossing dumbly through the night—
anxious to exorcize this dream
and rest in peace in my own bed—
I might not dread the morning light,

dread finding out what new assault
was launched in darkness from the sky
against whomever's next in line
to be disposed of.—So who's at fault,
then, these ecstatic birds, or I?
Cowering in my own design

of arrogance, hung up on the air,
I'm stuck, the victim of their song
(whether propaganda or prayer)
insisting nothing can go wrong,
and nothing I do can defy it.

Vince Gotera

Editor, North American Review. *Filipino-American poet. Poetry collections include* Dragonfly and Ghost Wars *(2003, an antiwar chapbook). Veteran, U.S. Army.*

Guard Duty

A young soldier squints into thick black night
hoping no hostile sapper is cutting through
barbed wire, a bayonet and grenades tied
to his waist . . . invisible. This mute scenario

lies at the heart of three generations' bedtime
stories: my Lolo and my Papa in the U.S.
Army, Philippine Scouts, death march in Bataan,
my brother Pepito in the 'Nam, nightmares

of Agent Orange. That young soldier could have been
any one of them . . . or me, on guard mount at Fort Ord
during Vietnam. Almost dreaming machine gun
recoil in our hands. Screaming, an oncoming horde.

Never again . . . young women and men should dream
of breezes in trees, soft rain, sunshine. Never again.

Michael Gould-Wartofsky

17 YEARS OLD
NEW YORK CITY
Michael Gould-Wartofsky is a high school student in New York City and founder of NY Youth Bloc. He has performed his work at the Nuyorican Poets Cafe and the Bowery Poetry Club.

Poetry of Bodies

I see a poetry of bodies
Bowed down to the ground, then
Rising to the sound of the beating of the heart of a heartless
    world that's
Starved for the sacred
And in another part of this parted world, boys and girls
    are starved and naked
Earth-scraping for something to stuff emaciated faces with
Verse taken by the grace of the Master Race when
Stumbling on the seeds of hatred, planted in forsaken places
Leaving generations vacant
Like the sand painted over with pavement, lands raped and
Red stripes in the wake of the acid rainmaking
There's no poetry in the bodies stacked in mass graves and
The bodies paying death's wages sitting on their ass
    complacent
Or marching with death without their goosestep breaking
But some bodies have awakened from the longest sleep
Bodies fully human, no longer belonging with sheep
I hear the living song as it leaps
From the bodies in the throngs up the steepest mountain
All along the peak resounding

A poetry of bodies seeping from the deepest fountain
   into the streets of our towns
To put down the sweeps of those with skin colored
   brown and
Drown the beat of the war drums' pound
And in the middle of winter, we've found the heat to
   surround

———

Marilyn Hacker

Marilyn Hacker is a National Book Award winner.

MORNING NEWS

Spring wafts up the smell of bus exhaust, of bread
and fried potatoes, tips green on the branches,
but it's old news: arrogance, ignorance, war.
A cinder-block wall shared by two houses
is new rubble. On one side was a kitchen
sink and a cupboard, on the other was
a bed, a bookshelf, three framed photographs.

Glass is shattered across the photographs;
two half-circles of
hardened pocket-bread
sit on the cupboard. There provisionally was
shelter, a plastic truck under the branches
of a fig-tree. A knife flashed in the kitchen,
merely dicing garlic. Engines of war
move inexorably towards certain houses

while citizens sit safe in other houses
reading the newspaper, whose photographs
give sanitized excuses for the war.
There are innumerable kinds of bread
brought up from bakeries, baked in the kitchen:
the date, the latitude, tell which one was
dropped by a child beneath the bloodied branches.

The uncontrolled and multifurcate branches
of possibility infiltrate houses'
walls, windowframes, ceilings. Where there was
a tower, a town: ash and burnt wires, a graph
on a distant computer screen. Elsewhere, a kitchen
table's setting gapes, where children bred
to branch into new lives were culled for war.

Who wore this starched smocked cotton dress? Who wore
this jersey blazoned for the local branch
of the district soccer team? Who left this black bread
and this flat gold bread in their abandoned houses?
Whose father begged for mercy in the kitchen?
Whose memory will frame the photograph
and use the memory for what it was

never meant for by this girl, that old man, who was
caught on a ball-field, near a window: war,
exhorted through the grief a photograph
revives (or was the team a covert branch
of a banned group; were maps drawn in the kitchen,
a bomb thrust in a hollowed loaf of bread?).
What did the old men pray for in their houses

of prayer, the teachers teach in schoolhouses
between blackouts and blasts, when each word was
flensed by new censure, books exchanged for bread,
both hostage to the happenstance of war?
Sometimes the only schoolroom is a kitchen.
Outside the window, black strokes on a graph
of broken glass, birds line up on bare branches.

"This letter curves, this one spreads its branches
like friends holding hands outside their houses."
Was the lesson stopped by gunfire, was
there panic, silence, does
a torn photograph
still gather children in the teacher's kitchen?
Are they there meticulously learning war-
time lessons with the signs for house, book, bread?

———

Pamela Hale
35 YEARS OLD
HOUSTON, TEXAS
I'm an ordinary person from an ordinary place.

Poem for an Iraqi Child in a Forgotten News Clip

I'm sorry that your mom was killed
When a missile struck your home
You were only three, and innocent.
Your mother too was innocent.

That missile came in my name,
Paid for by my tax dollars.
I was against the bombing, but
Not registered to vote,
Afraid to make a stand.

I have a daughter, about your age.
She is beautiful and strong.
Her mother is here, her father there,
But her home has never been bombed.

She makes fliers to pass out at school.
"No one should have to die for oil."
She scares her teachers and school counselor.
She is too young to vote.
But not afraid to make a stand.

This time, I will not stand idly by
While politicians propagandize and
Big corporations divvy up the booty
In advance. No.

This time I will make my voice heard,
Say the things I couldn't say before,
Support my daughter and the others when
They stand against another unjust war.

I am sorry for your loss.
Sorry too, for my part in it,
My apathy, my inattention.
Sorry for your loneliness and deprivation.
Your lost childhood. Your pain.

Sorry for the bombs that fell and fell,
For the planes that circle still.
In my name.

Sidney Hall, Jr.

52 YEARS OLD
BROOKLINE, NEW HAMPSHIRE
Poet, columnist and publisher.

Imagine

A word from a song,
Printed brightly on a blue banner
Hung on the highest balcony.

Impossible to imagine
A war that has not begun,
A black-headed boy buried
Along with his soccer ball,
A young mother's broken breast
On a red sidewalk.

A word from a song.

Impossible to imagine
One quarter of a million people
In the streets trying to end
A war that has not begun.

Impossible to imagine the echo
Of incensed humanity
Twisting up the avenue
Between the white buildings,
Or the face of a man next to me in the march,
Under a thick blue hood,
Behind a grey beard,
Crying as secretly as he can.

Elisabeth Hallett

55 YEARS OLD
HAMILTON, MONTANA
Mother; author of nonfiction and one book of poetry

Difficult to Sleep

Difficult to sleep this way
stretched over the doomed city
pinned down at eight hundred points
each point a planned calamity.
In the wide awake mind's eye
clay colored streets and houses
are a fading photograph
a stony mattress under me.

In the soon-to-be-ruined city
the fathers confer in code,
carefully handle chipped pieces

of their children's faith. The fathers say
Is it time to go to the orchards?
But already the sadness of children
saturates this film I am, silvery emulsion
that registers too much, too little.

Go to the orchards
although the fruit's unripe.
Apricots are hard, green knobs.
Retreat right back into the roots of the trees,
alien people: we don't know your names.
We haven't got your forwarding address.

———

Madeleine-Therese Halpert
9 YEARS OLD
ITHACA, NEW YORK
I play the cello and piano, dance and sing (and I have three brothers and two sisters).

from Maddie (age 9)

terror in their eyes
children now lost forever
Innocent, like me

———

Sam Hamill

PORT TOWNSEND, WASHINGTON
Sam Hamill is the co-founder of Copper Canyon Press and the founder and editor of Poets Against the War.

Sheepherder Coffee

I used to like sheepherder coffee,
a cup of grounds in my old enameled pot,
then three cups of water and a fire,

and when it's hot, boiling into froth,
a half cup of cold water
to bring the grounds to the bottom.

It was strong and bitter and good
as I squatted on the riverbank,
under the great redwoods, all those years ago.

Some days, it was nearly all I got.
I was happy with my dog,
and cases of books in my funky truck.

But when I think of that posture now,
I can't help but think
of Palestinians huddled in their ruins,

the Afghani shepherd with his bleating goats,
the widow weeping, sending off her sons,
the Tibetan monk who can't go home.

There are fewer names for coffee
than for love. Squatting, they drink,
thinking, waiting for whatever comes.

Patricia Hampl
MINNEAPOLIS, MINNESOTA

Statement of Conscience

Dear President Bush:

As a student during the Vietnam War, I read Walt
Whitman's poems almost obsessively in a desperate
effort to keep my love for my country alive and vivid
during that awful period. Now it seems everyone claims
to have been "against the war" in those years, but in fact,
as you probably remember too, those who opposed the
war were often vilified. Only time has brought about a
consensus of how ruinous that engagement was. Like
many Americans, I was devastated by what we were doing
in Southeast Asia, by the mayhem we caused there, and by
the disfiguration we brought to our own best selves at
home by our actions there.

My boyfriend and other friends of mine went to prison
rather than join that war. I became a poet in the midst of
that period, and my sense of poetry was rooted, from the
start, in a commitment to a national morality, not simply
to personal exploration or expression.

What you propose to do in the name of America and in the name of all its citizens carries an even heavier threat of disgrace and terror (for ourselves as well as the poorest of the world). I have made an effort to try to follow your reasoning, but I must confess the action you propose seems more and more insupportable.

Now, in these times which become increasingly desperate, I find myself turning again to a great poet for direction, clarity—and serenity. Not Whitman this time, but the great medieval Muslim Sufi poet, Rumi, whose tomb I visited only two years ago in Turkey—in other words, a poet of the very region now under threat. Here are two short poems by Rumi from the many thousands he wrote—so many that they are simply numbered, not titled. These versions are the work of John Moyne and Coleman Barks. I offer them to you in the spirit of peace—may it prevail:

#88
Today, like every other day, we wake up empty
and frightened. Don't open the door to the study
and begin reading. Take down the dulcimer.

Let the beauty we love be what we do.
There are hundreds of ways to kneel and kiss the ground.

#1616
Inside the Great Mystery that is,
we don't really own anything.

What is this competition we feel then,
before we go, one at a time, through the same gate?

Sincerely,
Patricia Hampl

———

Twyla Hansen
53 YEARS OLD
LINCOLN, NEBRASKA
*Poet and Horticulturist, from a long line of Danish farmers, from
women and men of the soil, all imperfect, all vulnerable and hard at
work. Latest book:* Potato Soup.

VETERANS DAY

By the time I came along the war was legend,
Its submerged evidence washed up for me to learn:
Mike's father with his flash-burned eyes, a first cousin
Dead at Pearl Harbor, the rag-tag veterans parade

At our hometown Decoration Day. I studied the shadow
Of cultural hatred, the philosophy of patriotic zeal.

Each year brought the cut opulence of common
Blooming things—flags, ferns, sickly-sweet peonies—

Each observance a raising of rifles and salutes,
The lingering of sulfur, the lonesomeness of taps.

But more than anything I tasted the sad luck of blood:
My father—too old for this war, too young for the first—

Exempt, suspended in that awkwardness of time,
Serving his country stuck in fields of corn and wheat,

His rank at the helm of a tractor, his hands grasping air
In the empty maneuvers of his unspoken grief.

———

Danielle Hanson

30 YEARS OLD

ATLANTA, GEORGIA

Danielle Hanson received her M.F.A. from Arizona State University. She is former poetry editor of Hayden's Ferry Review *and her work has appeared there, as well as in* Poetry Miscellany, Hiram Poetry Review, The Marlboro Review, The Lucid Stone, Willow Springs, Nebraska Review, Cimarron Review, Carriage House Review, *and* Sulphur River Literary Review.

Igneous

Tonight the goddess of love and war,
is spitting the wind in our direction.
Regardless, you light candles
as if to lose some sun before tomorrow,
as if to hold the past as smoldering match.
I am watching you hunt for the right words
and not to take you out of context
but someone has to take you
down this river. It's been more times
than I've stood on the shore feeling the earth move,
feeling the mountains being exhumed.
I looked to continental drift theory,
discovered the heat, the radioactive decay,
feeding those peaks of lava, tearing the ground apart
beneath us like a hawk.
I know that I've looked into those chasms
and seen you, that losing you
is forgetting love,
that it's the sharpest razor you cannot feel.

Joy Harjo
HONOLULU, HAWAII

Joy Harjo is the recipient of the American Indian Distinguished Acheivement in the Arts award and the William Carlos Williams award.

NO

Yes that was me you saw shaking with bravery, with a government issued rifle on my back. I'm sorry I could not greet you as you deserved, my relative.

No. They were not my tears. I have a reservoir inside. They will be cried by my sons, my daughters if I can't learn how to turn tears to stone.

Yes, that was me standing in the back door of the house in the alley, with a bowl of beans in my hands for the neighbors, a baby on my hip.

No. I did not foresee the flood of blood. How they would forget our friendship, would return to kill me and the baby.

Yes, that was me whirling on the dance floor. We made such a racket with all that joy. I loved the whole world in that silly music.

No. I did not realize the terrible dance in the staccato of bullets.

Yes. I smelled the burning grease of corpses after they were lit by the pages of our poems. And like a fool I expected our words might rise up and jam the artillery in the hands of dictators.

No. We had to keep going. Our songs of grief cleaned the air of enemy spirits.

Yes, I did see the terrible black clouds over the suburb as I cooked dinner. And the messages of the dying spelled there in the ashy sunset. Every one addressed: "mother".

No, there was nothing about it in the news. Everything was the same. Unemployment was up. Another queen crowned with flowers. Then there were the sports scores.

Yes, the distance was great between your country and mine. Yet our children played in the path between our houses.

We had no quarrel with each other.

———

Marie Harris

59 YEARS OLD
NEW HAMPSHIRE
Author of four books of poetry, a children's book and editor of several anthologies. New Hampshire poet laureate.

Sometimes the Wider World Can Only Be Apprehended Obliquely

Snakes are always all of a sudden, no matter where I encounter them. These two were baking under a sheet of black plastic that covered the old bales of mulch hay I needed for the onion row. A garter (imagine it wound in delicate coils about a stockinged thigh!) and another I can't name (silver-white core emblazoned along its length with brown ovals etched in delicate black). Exposed and surprised by light, uncoiling, they tongue the bright air. Spiders hurry away carrying bulging white sacs. Ants rearrange their ranks. There has been a profound disturbance. Each small movement occasions an intricate series of counter movements. I couldn't have predicted, for instance, the thousands of reactions to my shadow.

Jim Harrison

Jim Harrison is the winner of a National Endowment for the Arts grant and a Guggenheim fellowship.

Poem of War

The old rancher of seventy-nine years
    said while branding and nutting young bulls
     with the rank odor of burned hairs and flesh
    in the air, the oil slippery red nuts
    plopping into a galvanized bucket,
     "this smells just like Guadalcanal."

––––––

    The theocratic cowboy forgetting Viet Nam rides
into town on a red horse. He's praying to himself
    not God, though the two are confused
   in the heat of vengeance. The music
  is the thump of derricks, the computerized
    lynch mob geek dissonance. Clint Eastwood
    whispers from an alley, "George, they
were only movies." Shock and Awe.
  God is only on God's side. War prayers
    swim in their tanks of pus like poisoned
     frogs in algae laden ponds. The red horse
    he rides is the horse of blasphemy. Jesus
     leads a flower laden donkey across the Red Sea
    in the other direction, his nose full of the stink
   of corpses. Buddha and Mohammed offer
cool water from a palm's shade while young
   men die in the rocket's red glare
    and in the old men's hard peckered dreams.

Acknowledgements

Thanks to the following who made this book possible:

Board of Directors—Sally Anderson, Gray Foster, Sam Hamill, Andrew Himes, Peter Lewis and Nancy Scott.

Special Projects—Nancy Giebink, Jonathan King, Craig Kosak, Mary Lathrop and Joel Leskowitz.

Web Development & Content Team—Tom Blumer, David Habib, Nina Kang andSamantha Moscheck.

PAW Website Editors—Sally Anderson, Kelly Blue, Otts Bolisay, Jan Bultmann, David Caligiuri, Ina Chang, Hugo Cuevas, Carolyn Hauck, Nancy Johnson, Pam Kilborn-Miller, Jonathan King, Karen Lenburg, Jim Molnar, Brenda Matteson, Tom McDonald, Olga Owens, Mary Park, Joseph Riley, Ellen Setteducati, Holly Thomas, Ken Thompson, Lori Walls, Michael Welch, Jessamyn West and Alix Wilber.

Assistance in Washington, DC—Jill Bond, Sarah Browning CodePink, Kim Roberts, Sandy Solomon, Emily Warn.

Featured Readers—Cornelius Eady, W. S. Merwin and Terry Tempest Williams.

Miscellaneous—Carrie Demming, Tim Feeder, Jeff Hayward, Amy Schaus Murphy and Ward Serrill.

Poetry Reading Coordinators, Seattle—Mary Lathrop, Ellen Setteducati, Michael Welch.

U.S. Representatives—Marcy Kaptur (D-Ohio), Dennis Kucinich (D-Ohio), Jim McDermott (D-Washington).

With special thanks to the extraordinary poets who spoke out at readings around the world, and to everyone who submitted a poem, sent a donation, or otherwise showed support at such an important and perilous junction in history.

René Char asked, "Who stands on the gangplank
directing operations, the captain or the rats?"
Whitman said, "so many young throats
choked on their own blood." God says nothing.

February 13, 2003

———

Samuel Hazo

I am the state poet of the Commonwealth of Pennsylvania, Distinguished McAnulty Professor Emeritus at Duquesne University in Pittsburgh, and director of the International Poetry Forum.

E-mail for Sam

Dear Sam,

I received your email request for a poem. I too saw the "Shock and Awe" segment (400 cruise missiles the first day, 300 the next and so on), and I was appalled by the cold-blooded calmness of the official who was dispassionately describing the attack and its human toll. I'll be proud to be associated with you in this timely and important project, and I am sending the enclosed as my contribution.

BALLAD OF A DISSENTER

THE PRESIDENT SPEAKS ABOUT GOVERNMENT LEAKS
AS IF STATING THE TRUTH IS A BLUNDER.

BUT WHO SAYS IT'S WRONG IF YOU DON'T GO
   ALONG
NO MATTER HOW MANY MAY WONDER?

AND WHEN WAS IT RIGHT TO BE BLIND IN PLAIN SIGHT
WHILE THE FACTS ARE OUT THERE FOR THE SAYING?
BUT MUM IS THE NAME OF THE PRESIDENT'S GAME,
AND ONLY THE FAVORED ARE PLAYING.

WHOEVER'S THE FIRST TO IMAGINE THE WORST
IS SURE TO BE SCORNED AND DERIDED.
BUT ONLY THE FREE SHALL SAY WHAT THEY SEE
ON AN ISSUE THAT'S MORE THAN ONE-SIDED.

BEFORE YOU SPOKE OUT, YOU RARELY WOULD
   DOUBT
THE NEWS OF EACH DAY AND THEREAFTER.
BUT HOW YOU'RE ALONE WITH A MIND OF YOUR
   OWN,
AND YOUR VIEWS ARE APPLAUDED WITH LAUGHTER.

IT'S ONE THING TO DREAM OF THE TIMES AS THEY
   SEEM.
IT'S QUITE SOMETHING ELSE TO AWAKEN
WITH RAGE ON YOUR TONGUE WHEN YOU'RE NO
   LONGER YOUNG
AND TO LEARN THAT YOUR DREAM WAS MISTAKEN.

—

Allison Hedge Coke

44 years old
Sioux Falls, South Dakota
American Book Award, 1997. Full-time literary artist in residence, Sioux Falls. Adjunct, University of Sioux Falls, S.D. Arts Alliance Board, Arts Corr, Touring Arts, former caucus member Wordcraft Circle of Native Writers and Storytellers, former board member American Indian Registry of Performing Arts.

swarming

swarming upward
hosts thicken air as hornets
with whirling winds
their weapons wielded wildly

back home blackbirds whirl
in skies greyed
from icy winter chill, frost,
a single sparrow cowers against
bush base huddling

wind bristles with his war
skies hustle
fields, valleys, meadows moan
mountains reel
all creatures
cater to whims of man
in chaotic frenzy for battle
when peace is ever present
in just one thoughtful breath

breathe, breathe deep

Brenda Hillman

GREEN PANTS AND A BAMBOO FLUTE

Oaks tear up the storm floor
Nothing left to warn
The poisoned rat has poisoned the owl
The striped air of the state is choked
With pointed salty star materials
They've cut the tips off dollar bills
Now chipped stars everywhere seems like
Death planes with Daisy Chains
Bombs with cute little names
Swordfish stab the water's skin
The sea has no plot

Earlier thinkers thought of air
As a mist not a context
With each bomb the part
That was narrow shrinks.
Our god passes by briefly
From another existence
With his pretty floating rib
The one they call the twelfth
The webbed arch of caravans
Frames the desert horror
The owl's eyes follow them
On this side of the pale

One night in a vision
Your future car was buried
Today you drive the buried car
Turn like a three-part song

Electricity wants not to be anymore
Or to be darktricity
The brain is an atmosphere of rooms
A situation without a future
Where *us* presides over an it
The doom's-whim-bride's-trace fog
Doubles as a shroud

If the flute cannot be found
Its breath is in you
Making an @ sign of sex or grain
What was it thinking of
The catkins look so like grenades
Maybe the particle spirits
Will spin in the at of each address
Knock the wheel of fate from its orbit
Race to a curled up
Solomon's sleep in the clock's
Ring moist with air

Jane Hirshfield

Jane Hirshfield's honors include the Poetry Center Book Award and a Guggenheim fellowship.

The Dead Do Not Want Us Dead

The dead do not want us dead;
such petty errors are left for the living.
Nor do they want our mourning.
No gift to them—not rage, not weeping.
Return one of them, any one of them, to the earth,
and look: such foolish skipping,
such telling of bad jokes, such feasting!
Even a cucumber, even a single anise seed: feasting.

———

Tony Hoagland

The Kind of Shadow That Calls Out Fate

Early in the day reports said our planes
had bombed a wedding in a distant country—

We could tell it had really happened
from the way the spokespersons on TV hesitated

before denying it—from the way they cleared their throats
and said it was pending investigation.

You know those crazy natives and their customs,
well, apparently it was their way of celebration
          to shoot their rifles into the air

and jets showed up soon afterwards—forty dead,
and some of them horses.

Hearing about it over and over through the week
hearing the descriptions repeated over and over

of the colorful wedding clothes made brighter by the
  blood
the groans coming from the dying bride,

the bad news surrounded our house, like something rotten:
We sensed we couldn't get away with this one.

It was exactly the sort of thing which in a Greek play
would initiate a sequence of events

that turns inexorably back to bite
the hand that set it into motion

—and we knew we also were part of the plot.
We sat there in the audience as we have so often

as at a scene where the king drops his crown
which rolls across the floor and falls offstage

while he scrambles after it
—and thoughtfully, the queen watches.

Patricia Ikeda

49 YEARS OLD
OAKLAND, CALIFORNIA
Patricia Ikeda also writes under her Buddhist and married name, Mushim Ikeda-Nash. A graduate of the Iowa Graduate Writers' Workshop, she is currently a socially engaged Buddhist activist in the Bay Area.

Anniversary

1
End of summer and
orchards sell peaches so ripe
welts crack open, wet mouths.
The clear juice
perfumes the kitchen.

Today's the anniversary,
the newspaper says.
This first week in August
tourists come in droves,
shopkeepers set out displays.

I spoon bits of
ripe peach into pies, rinse
the clear glass bowl.

2
Anniversary,
the paper says,
Hiroshima

"a hole in history"

3
Breeze from the west
riffles the curtains. Pies
on the counter, small things
and large all sliding
toward the glowing clouds,
eaten away. I
turn on the faucet, lift
a glass of water
turned red, turned round
and big as fire.

———

Kent Johnson
47 YEARS OLD
FREEPORT, ILLINOIS
Kent Johnson's most recent book is Immanent Visitor: Selected
Poems of Jaime Saenz, *which he translated with Forrest Gander.*

Baghdad

Oh, little crown of iron forged to likeness of imam's face,
what are you doing in this circle of flaming inspectors
    and bakers?

And little burnt dinner all set to be eaten
(and crispy girl all dressed with scarf for school),
what are you doing near this shovel for dung-digging,
hissing like ice-cubes in ruins of little museum?

And little shell of bank on which flakes of assets fall,
can't I still withdraw my bonds for baby?

Good night moon.
Good night socks and good night cuckoo clocks.

Good night little bedpans and a trough where once there
    was an inn
(urn of dashed pride),
what are you doing beside little wheelbarrow
beside some fried chickens?

And you, ridiculous wheels spinning on mailman's truck,
truck with ashes of letter from crispy girl all dressed with
    scarf for school,
why do you seem like American experimental poets
    going nowhere
on little exercise bikes?

Good night barbells and ballet dancer's shoes
under plastered ceilings of Saddam Music Hall.

Good night bladder of Helen Vendler and a jar from
    Tennessee.
(though what are these doing here in Baghdad?)

Good night blackened ibis and some keys.
Good night, good night.

(And little mosque popped open like a can, which same
    as factory of flypaper has blown outward, covering the-
    shape of man with it (with mosque): He stumbles up
    Martyr's Promenade. What does it matter who is

speaking, he murmurs and mutters, head a little bit on
fire. Good night to you too.)

Good night moon.
Good night poor people who shall inherit the moon.

Good night first editions of Das Kapital, Novum Organum,
The Symbolic Affinities between Poetry Blogs and Oil Wells,
and the Koran.

Good night nobody.

Good night Mr. Kent, good night, for now you must
soon wake up and rub your eyes and know that you are
    dead.

———

Frank Judge

The Monument

This will be the final
war—one unexpected
morning a hand will
move a moment too soon,
the moment will spin out of hand
and the sands will turn
into a great lake of glass
covering cities and citizens,
transforming them

like the stone residents
of Pompeii and Herculaneum
but as visible as insects in amber.

For a while it will be
a monument twice
the size of Texas
requiring special shoes
to tour. Then, after the
thermonuclear briefcases,
the sarin and VX, the
infected water, the viruses
drifting across continents
in wondrous patterns
only the dead can see,
snow will settle silently over
the false ice in the dark
afternoons of final victory.

The museum will be free
of charge, open all the days
and weeks of the world
to pilgrimages of ghosts.

Shirley Kaufman

The Last Threshold

I want to believe we still talk about
Peace
             as if it were out there somewhere
an illumination in more Xmas card languages
than anyone speaks

             "eventually"
won't come for me to see it

Deborah writes
             We all live in a
morally ambiguous vortex

but the rough beast is done
with his slouching
             Bush is massing
his troops for the kill
our dinosaur generals are ready

they are used to the rivers
of blood
             that weep from dismembered bodies
             that howl in the streets of Ramallah
             that shriek in the streets of Jerusalem

                    February 27, 2003
                    Jerusalem

Galway Kinnell

Galway Kinnell's Selected Poems *was awarded the Pulitzer Prize and the National Book Award.*

The Olive Wood Fire

When Fergus woke crying at night
I would carry him from his crib
to the rocking chair and sit holding him
before the fire of thousand-year-old olive wood.
Sometimes, for reasons I never knew
and he has forgotten, even after his bottle the big tears
would keep on rolling down his big cheeks
—the left cheek always more brilliant than the right—
and we would sit, some nights for hours, rocking
in the light eking itself out of the ancient wood,
and hold each other against the darkness,
his close behind and far away in the future,
mine I imagined all around.
One such time, fallen half-asleep myself,
I thought I heard a scream
—a flier crying out in horror
as he dropped fire on he didn't know what or whom,
or else a child thus set aflame—
and sat up alert. The olive wood fire
had burned low. In my arms lay Fergus,
fast asleep, left cheek glowing, God.

Mallorca, winter 1970.

Carolyn Kizer

Carolyn Kizer has received many awards including the Frost Medal.

Gulf War

Tout le ciel vert se meurt.
Le dernier arbre brûle.
                    —Valery

The whole green sky is dying. The last tree flares.
With a great burst of supernatural rose
Under a canopy of poisonous airs.

Could we imagine our return to prayers
To end in time before time's final throes,
The green sky is dying as the last tree flares?

But we were young in judgement, old in years
Who could make peace: but it was war we chose,
To spread its canopy of poisoning airs.

Not all our children's pleas and women's fears
Could steer us from this hell. And now God knows
His whole green sky is dying as it flares.

Our crops of wheat have turned to fields of tares
This dreadful century staggered to its close
And the sky dies for us, its poisoned heris.

All rain was dust. Its granules were out of tears.
Throats burst as universal winter rose
To kill the whole green sky, the last tree bare
Beneath its canopy of poisoned air.

Maxine Kumin

77 YEARS OLD
WARNER, NEW HAMPSHIRE
Author of thirteen collections of poems, a memoir, three essay collections, etc. Winner of Pulitzer and Ruth Lilly Awards, pro-choice, antiVietnam & this impending war.

New Hampshire, February 7, 2003

It's snowing again.
All day, reruns
of the blizzard of '78
newscasters vying
for bragging rights
how it was to go hungry
after they'd thumped
the vending machines empty
the weatherman clomping
four miles on snowshoes
to get to his mike
so he could explain
how three lows
could collide to create
a lineup of isobars
footage of state troopers
peering into the caked
windows of cars
backed up for white
miles on the interstate.

Nowhere, reruns
of the bombings in Vietnam
2 million civilians blown

apart, most of them children
under 16, children
always the least
able to dive
for cover when
all that tonnage bursts
from a blind sky.
Snow here is
weighting the pine trees
while we wait for the worst:
for war to begin.
Schools closed, how
the children
love a benign blizzard
a downhill scrimmage
of tubes and sleds. But who
remembers the blizzard
that burst on those other children?
Back then we called it
collateral damage
and will again.

Stanley Kunitz

97 YEARS OLD
NEW YORK CITY
Stanley Kunitz's collection Passing Through *was awarded the National Book Award and his* Selected Poems *won the Pulitzer Prize.*

Statement

Mr. President,

In the name of humanity and common decency, the poets of "this nation of nations," as Walt Whitman defined the country that we cherish, implore you not to launch a so-called "pre-emptive" strike against the subject people of Iraq. Have you reckoned with the consequences, the danger of inciting World War III?

When they shall paint our sockets gray
And light us like a stinking fuse,
Remember that we once could say,
Yesterday we had a world to lose.

Stephen Kuusisto
47 years old
Columbus, Ohio

Wartime Radio

Winter has my neighbors
By the throat—
The collective throat.

Deep in the Ohio
River Valley
Everyone's poor.

The drug store
Is boarded up
And Amish carpenters

Tear down a barn.
The President
Calls for war

While the police
Hand out coats
Beside a field stove.

The sky
Leans
Without mercy.

Dorianne Laux
OREGON

CELLO

When a dead tree falls in a forest
it often falls into the arms
of a living tree. The dead,
thus embraced, rasp in wind,
slowly carving a niche
in the living branch, sheering away
the rough outer flesh, revealing
the pinkish, yellowish, feverish
inner bark. For years
the dead tree rubs its fallen body
against the living, building
its dead music, making its raw mark,
wearing the tough bough down,
moaning in wind, the deep
rosined bow sound of the living
shouldering the dead.

September, 2002

Ursula K. Le Guin

Portland, Oregon

Ursula K. Le Guin is well known for her science fiction and has won the National Book Award.

American Wars

Like the topaz in the toad's head
the comfort in the terrible histories
was up front, easy to find:
Once upon a time in a kingdom far away.

Even to the dreadful now of news
we listened comforted
by far timezones, languages we didn't speak,
the wide, forgetful oceans.

Today, no comfort but the jewel courage.
The war is ours, now, here, it is our republic
facing its own betraying terror.
And how we tell the story is forever after.

Peter Levitt

Statement of Conscience

Thank you so much for organizing this. In support of all my poetry brothers and sisters rising up against a war being fought against our will but in our name I gratefully offer the following:

For a poet, whose morality and word are identities, there is often nothing more substantial to place against the cruelty of the world than the innate intimacy between things a poem manages to express. I think that as poets we have the hidden hope—perhaps hidden even from ourselves—that, against all odds, our poems will somehow reestablish a ground where life, in all its true nature and various forms, can live as it was meant to. Foolish, foolish souls, blessed with the notion—the certainty—that a human being armed with nothing more than a syllable may help to repair the world. And yet, if only for a moment here and there, we have not been proven wrong.

untitled

Fill the air with poems
so thick—
even bombs
can't fall through

Morton Marcus

Tale of A Doorknob

A lieutenant salutes his major, nods to an enlisted man who triggers a heavy artillery piece. Five miles away, a child hugging a rag doll closes an apartment door behind her as the door, apartment, whole building collapses before she can remove her hand from the knob. She will be found that way in the rubble, gripping the round piece of metal she had turned in the door countless times on the mornings she went out to play or run to the store for her mother—overcast mornings, sunny mornings, mornings filled with rain.

The soldiers will wonder at the little girl without a face who lies ten feet away from the remains of a rag doll, still holding a round metal object that looks like a doorknob. Several of them will stare, several others will turn away or throw up or curse the hills, the enemy, the war, even the perfidy of humankind. Invaders or defenders, their reactions will be the same.

Only two or three—a general, a sergeant, a private— will be struck by the thought that the girl is holding what could be a globe of the world, or some other symbolic shape, and one of them will gently, or not so gently, pry her fingers open to retrieve the object and bring it home to his children as a souvenir, accompanying the gift with tales of conquest in a foreign country, or with instructions for merciless vengeance in his own land.

Statement of Conscience

In recent years I've known that I was getting old because things that happened thirty or forty years ago were happening again, especially corruption in high places going unpunished, lack of concern for the economic and social plight of middle-and low-income citizens, and our blind embracing of war with Iraq under the pretext of patriotism. The latter, under the guise of fighting terrorism, has even less legitimacy than our embroilment in Vietnam. I am a Korean vet and a lover of America, a patriot, but one who has thought that America was promises that have not yet been kept and now seem farther away than ever. The pursuit of this war and our unilateral stance on a number of world issues have left me saddened and depressed. The President and his administration have proven again and again that they lack the two elements of great leadership—empathy and compassion. This is not a poem. These events, especially the administration's war-mongering, have sucked the poetry out of me.

Karen Margalit

50 YEARS OLD
BERLIN
Born Harare, lived in South Africa and London, degree in mathematics from London School of Economics, 1974. Live and work in Berlin since 1983. Published works include co-author Technology of Political Control, To Eat or Not to Eat, *essays and poems.*

Writing my diary with water

inspired by a work of art by Song Dong
Chinese art exhibition, Berlin, September 2001

I'm writing my diary with water
to wash away my fears
dipping the pen in water
to drown the flood of tears

the water runs into the words
blurring the green scrawls of hope
I'm writing a diary of slaughter
in a battle where I can't cope

I'll give up pen and paper
find an unmarked stone in a field
smooth a space upon its face
and ask my thoughts to yield

I'll dip the brush in water
write poems on the stone
they'll soak in till they're watermarks

an epitaph for me alone

Gary Margolis

57 YEARS OLD
MIDDLEBURY, VERMONT
Gary Margolis is director of the center of counseling and Human Relations at Middlebury College.

The Palace of Lists

Where are we
hiding our
weapons
of the heart?
In the heartland
or here, in the north,
where the racked deer—
those tan harts—
are safe until next
November?
Where is the list
we are expected
to disclose that
comes closest
to what we feel
when we see a deer
hanging from a maple
branch, gutted and
curing, when we can't
say what we think?
How far into the palace
of lists do we walk
before we find our room
of fear, its walls hung

with rugs, stories of
the kill woven into
their threads?
How long will it take
to know what we are told
must be there, chambered
and ready to be known?
Even that six-pointed buck
can tell what we have eaten
when the wind pulls us
into his knowing
and there is nothing
between us except
the unafraid air.

William Marr

66 YEARS OLD
CHICAGO

William Marr was born in Taiwan in 1936 and received his Ph.D. degree in nuclear engineering from the University of Wisconsin. He has published thirteen volumes of poetry in his native Chinese language. His recent book of selected poems, Autumn Window, *is in English. His poems have been translated into several languages and are included in numerous anthologies. He has also edited several anthologies of modern Taiwanese and Chinese poetry. He is a past president of the Illinois State Poetry Society, and a member of the Poets' Club of Chicago.*

Memorial Day

At Arlington, someone
Unknown goes down

The thousands, the thousands
Who have gone down in faraway fields
But who won't die in the heart—
How do we bury
The thousands

RJ McCaffery

30 YEARS OLD
ATHENS
RJ McCaffery is the editor of Eye Dialect (www.contemporary poetry.com/dialect)

The Peace Bell

I stand bare-handed at the door of the bell.
My fingers flutter across its gnarl
wrought from a truckload of luck-kissed coins and medals.

My knuckle: a soft tock on a gulf.
My fist half thrown: a tunk, not even a grave note.

Against the bell's heavy hang, I manage
a salvo of knocks for the ignorant living,
a scrabble of nails for the dead.

Janet McCann

60 YEARS OLD
TEXAS

I'm a Texas poet interested in animal welfare and issues concerning older women.

Snow Women

The voice is cold
reading your poem
in the cold air.

the dazzle of the winter mind
winces off the blackened ice.

no misery. but it is always there
as they ship the bodies back
from where the eager generals
sent the men-children,
our wrinkled helpless hands
twist and twist the knotted handkerchief.

can we do nothing, can we make nothing happen?

our no will turn to silence,
outshouted, overruled.
our silence to acquiescence,
even to participation.
unless we build a wall of balk that holds,
a wall of hands
to hold against the break.

nothing comes of silence,
snow women move nothing.
unless the wall hold,
the weak moth of will
flutter in the glare,
flare an ashy arc,
a comet for old women.

Wilden McIntosh-Round

7 YEARS OLD
WILSON, WYOMING

Wilden has always loved words since he was old enough to start using them. He's in the second grade. After attending a peace rally here in Jackson Hole a month or so ago, he was up in his room one evening after supper, quietly working . . .

Peace On The Land We Live On

Our Earth was created for us to live in peace on
And now, we are destroying our only home
For at this very moment
We could be working out problems
Telling people what they did that disappointed others
When we could be happy
And have our own blood
Flow in our own bodies
When we let it flow on the ground
And discuss disappointments in violence and war

Let this be the day
When our nation will be peaceful
And when brother and sister
Will discuss problems
Instead of fighting about them
This is our Planet
Our Earth

———

Lucie McKee

70 YEARS OLD
BENNINGTON, VERMONT
Poems have appeared in the Southern Review, Puerto del Sol, *the* Bennington Review, *the* Café Review. *A prose memoir of Ruth Stone appeared in* Paintbrush 2000/2001.

Denial

Today we are quite light—levitated by
mild caffeine. The sky is blue, the air is
still warm this early autumn day. But
it's getting somber in the west. So I look
east as long as I can. Look east as long as
the sun lasts, keep looking east as the
dust clouds sneak in behind me—look east
as the pale yolk slowly mixes with grimy
sewer water—Look east for as long as
any sky is blue. Then, I set up my easel
and paint blue sky until window light mixes

all my colors into dark gray. Switch on
a lamp in my house: *What a fine, sunny day.*
When the power goes out I crawl under
the bed, read about Spain with a flashlight.

———

Susan McKeon-Steinmann

58 YEARS OLD
LONG ISLAND, NEW YORK

I am a person who fought against the war in Vietnam for years and years and years. After leaving school I became a NYC school teacher, and retired after teaching almost thirty years. I never stopped working for peace and justice. That doesn't make me naive, as some claim. All this time I have written on old paper bags, napkins, leaflet-othersides. Whatever was handy. It was my writing that kept me focused. Someday it will not be a dream, there will be peace in the world because the evolved people of the world will not allow otherwise.

The seeds of the peace martyrs have borne fruit

We stand in the early nipping chill handing flyers to
    bleary-eyed commuters running for the train.
Ronkonkama, the name a left-over from our native past.
Will our culture be a left-over? as more and more
of our rights get taken in the name of the Homeland.

My homeland is here in the shadow of pine trees, in
    Wading River in darkness as the peace candles flicker.
My homeland all races and beliefs standing along
    Nicolls Road in Setauket,

signs as cars flash by, Honk for peace, the peace sign is
   given and the finger.
My homeland is in Northport with the flute player for
   peace, in Coram in front of the congressional office, It
stands in Sag Harbor mourning in black with the women,
My homeland is in the streets of Washington standing in
   the shadow of Martin and Fannie Lou Hamer, and
   Father Berrigan,
Citizens with heart refusing to accept thousands killed,
   tens of thousands made sick,
hundreds of thousands, millions living in terror
in the name of an American Imperial policy.
and I feel not one child, not one soldier is worth
the usurpation of someone else's oil field.

We are on a ship of state, careening wildly
toward disaster, taking us to an unknown destructive future,
There are mutinous feelings in the hearts of many.
The captain has gone mad.

———

Bridget Meeds
33 YEARS OLD
ITHACA, NEW YORK
Bridget Meeds is a poet and secretary from Ithaca, NY.

Letter to Hayden

Syracuse Sky Chiefs vs. the Scranton–Wilkes-Barre Red
Barons, P & C Stadium, Syracuse, NY, July 7, 2002

Hayden, the artificial turf at this new stadium
is a blinding petro-chemical green,
but the city planners still can't cover up
the sewage reek of Onondaga Lake,
my omphalos, stolen from the Iroquois,
a glimmering wound oozing with industrial pus.

Joe-Anne called from Munnsville to say
you are laid up on oxygen 24/7,
and I am picturing you on your hospital bed,
looking at your hillside and your apple tree
while the ballgame plays on your big TV,

and Hayden, don't worry,
Kavanagh wrote his longest lines
with half a lung,
and besides, I'm still young
and I've got breath enough
for the both of us,

and as far as I can reckon, Hayden,
baseball is a beautiful game,

and America is a beautiful country,
but from where I sit right now,
it stinks.

David Meltzer

From: SHEMA

Each word
the word
protecting life

all else
like bayonets
goes against it

in death's ink
sit soldiers
wrapping the dead
in book pages

the book weeps
black blood
in their mouths

the book weeps
white nerve thread
sewing dead eyes shut

the book weeps itself
empty of words

the book
a powder
like bone ash
warriors paint their faces with
to attack children

each word
the word
creating
protecting life
in lights of song
or silence

all else
goes against it

W. S. Merwin

75 YEARS OLD
HAWAII

W. S. Merwin's honors include the Aiken Taylor Award for Modern American Poetry, the Bollingen Prize, a Ford Foundation grant, the Governor's Award for Literature of the State of Hawaii, the Ruth Lilly Poetry Prize, the PEN Translation Prize, the Shelley Memorial Award, the Wallace Stevens Award, and a Lila Wallace–Reader's Digest Writers' Award, and fellowships from the Academy of American Poets, the Guggenheim Foundation, the National Endowment for the Arts, and the Rockefeller Foundation. He is a former chancellor of the Academy of American Poets and recently began a five-year term as judge of the Yale Series of Younger Poets.

Statement of Conscience

It would not have been possible for me ever to trust someone who acquired office by the shameful means Mr. Bush and his abettors resorted to in the last presidential election. His nonentity was rapidly becoming more apparent than ever when the catastrophe of September 11, 2001, provided him and his handlers with a role for him, that of "wartime leader", which they, and he in turn, were quick to exploit. This role was used at once to silence all criticism of the man and his words as unpatriotic, and to provide the auspices for a sustained assault upon civil liberties, environmental protections, and general welfare. The perpetuation of this role of "wartime leader" is the primary reason—more important even than the greed for oil fields and the wish to blot out his father's failure—for the present determination to visit war upon Iraq, kill and maim countless people, and antagonize much of the world of which Mr. Bush had not heard until recently. The real iniquities of Saddam Hussein should be recognized, in this context, as the pretexts they are. His earlier atrocities went unmentioned as long as he was an ally of former Republican administrations, which were happy, in their time, to supply him with weapons. I think that someone who was maneuvered into office against the will of the electorate, as Mr. Bush was, should be allowed to make no governmental decisions (including judicial appointments) that might outlast his questionable term, and if the reasons for war were many times greater than they have been said to be I would oppose anything of the kind under such "leadership." To arrange a war in order to be re-elected outdoes even the means employed in the last presidential election. Mr. Bush and hisplans are a greater danger to the United States than Saddam Hussein.

Ogres

All night waking to the sound
of light rain falling softly
through the leaves in the quiet
valley below the window
and to Paula lying here
asleep beside me and to
the murmur beside the bed
of the dogs' snoring like small
waves coming ashore I

am amazed at the fortune
of this moment in the whole
of the dark this unspoken
favor while it is with us
this breathing peace and then I
think of the frauds in office
at this instant devising
their massacres in my name
what part of me could they have
come from were they made of my
loathing itself and dredged from
the bitter depths of my shame

Jane Miller

A Palace of Pearls (excerpt)

Do you know how long it has been since a moral choice
  presented itself

and the wrong choice was made

not two minutes

why is it not quiet between lightning and thunder as if
  someone were asking

do you have other articulable feelings if so express them
  now

tragedy ensues

with a laser blast from the cockpit

the dangled finger of God makes contact

PLEASE CALL FOR SEVERAL HUNDRED THOUSAND
  PHYSICIANS QUICKLY

Mario Milosevic

"Suicide Note" originally appeared in Dreams and Nightmares #63, *September 2002.*

Suicide Note

The plaque on the Pioneer spacecraft
that was designed
to tell extra-terrestrials
all about us could easily outlive us.

Then the centerpiece of the design,
the naked woman standing beside the naked
            man,
his hand raised in a bland greeting,
both of them exposed to the elements
in a way that testifies to their indifference,
could easily be interpreted as a man saying
            good-bye
while his one true love stands with him,
perhaps saying good-bye in her own way.

Eons after the last human has died,
this image might be found
and read as the last act of life,
stuffed into the bottle of a spaceship
and sent into the sea of the cosmos
saying we had it all
we could have lived forever
but there was something in us
that we could not help
which just wanted everything to die.

Patricia Monaghan
DePaul University, Chicago, Illinois

THE WOMAN OF BAGDAD

She rises in the glow of a red sun
to make strong coffee. She fills her
cup with sugar from the bowl
her grandmother used. She sits
drinking slowly, beneath her lime tree.

I can see her through the blue glow
of the news: she moves with deliberate
grace in the silence of her morning.
As she reaches up to pull her hair
back from her neck, I see the tiny age
spots beginning on the back of her hand.

Men are talking somewhere, but she
does not hear them. She hears the murmur
of a dove in the tree. She hears the tiny
roar of a city wakening. She hears her heart
as we all hear ours, a soundless sound.

The men are saying she will die. The men
are saying the bombs are coming.
She, hearing nothing, gets up heavily
and picks a single lime from her tree.
She breathes its oily fragrance. These
are the last breaths she will take.

Grace Monte de Ramos

46 YEARS OLD
MANDALUYONG CITY, PHILIPPINES

I am a feminist poet raising two young children full-time. I read about this Web site only today, in an article by Charles Levendosky that was reprinted by one of Manila's newspapers. This submission is late for your deadline, but this act is a protest against the stupidity and parochial policies of the Bush administration.

Brave Woman

I am a mother of sons.
Two joined the army when they were young;
There was not enough money for school,
They had no skills for jobs in foundries
And factories, and it was easy to sign up
And learn how to handle a gun.

I am a mother of sons, two sons
And one, the youngest, now gone.
In his youth he was taken
By men whose names I never will learn.
I only know they were soldiers, like my sons,
Cradling fearsome guns.
He was a fine young man. I took care of him
For seventeen years and they took him away
And now I am searching for his bones.

I will never learn their names.
Alone I try to imagine the scene: were their faces
Bearded or clean-shaven?
Perhaps their bodies were robust.

Did they wear uniforms the color of shrivelled
Sampaguita or fresh horseshit?
How pointed the bullets from their guns?

My soldier sons come home
When life in the barracks is still.
I hide their brother's picture;
It makes them cry and remember.
Perhaps they, too (God forbid it),
Have given other mothers sorrow.
Perhaps my son had to pay for what they borrowed.

I cannot cry, though I am told
It is better to cry and let go.
Where is my son's body for me to bury?
I only wear my grief in the lines
Of my face, my sunken cheeks.
Silent, I mourn a woman's
Bitter lot: to give birth to men
Who kill and are killed.

Kaye Moon Winters

55 YEARS OLD
SEABROOK, TEXAS

I have been professionally writing, selling, and reciting original poetry in programs around the country for a number of years. In May 2000 I did so in Dallas, receiving praise for my poetry and performance from the keynote speaker, General Colin Powell. I received information about your movement in late January . . . just after I had written this poem. I was afraid to send it to you for I was frightened by its . . . truth. Today I read in the paper of First Lady Laura Bush's cancellation of a poetry event at the White House, reason given she feared some of the poets attending would attempt to politicize it. I knew at once the error I had made. I belatedly and contritely submit my poetic voice to your noble cause and offer my time and talents to your endeavor.

The Truth As I See It . . . Circa 2003

We're all too fat and we're all too rich
and all we do is whine and bitch
about the risin' cost of a tank of gas
while we boast to the world, "We'll kick yer ass
if you don't do just what we say
'cuz ours is the one and only way
and if you're good we'll let you pray
jest not in schools or at public games
'cuz if you do we'll take yer names
and add 'em to our growin' list
of folks who just don't git the gist
of what is comin' down the pike...
we don't give a damn what you like
'cuz we control all information
fed to every race and nation

and like sacrificial lambs, you'll die
unless you start to wonder . . .
Why . . . ?

Why do so many hate us so?
Why does any government have to know
what plants you eat or smoke or grow
and where and how you spend your time
and every single, shiny dime
and every call you ever make
and what you give and what you take and
Why . . . ?
at the dawn of 2003
is
war
once again our destiny?
As written in our history pages
on and on throughout the ages . . .
beating up on friend or foe
foments fears that grotesquely grow.
Compassion coupled with respect
for self and others will beget
a better path for all to walk,
with first step taken when you talk
one human being to another . . .
under One God . . . and of all other.

Melinda Mueller

49 YEARS OLD
SEATTLE, WASHINGTON
I am a high school biology teacher and poet.

LEDGER

"Does the air we vanish into taste of us, then?"
Second Duino Elegy
—Rainer Maria Rilke

1.
Suppose each star were named.
Suppose as each burnt down to cinders
someone mourned.
Suppose each scrap of paper
swirling through the streets
sang like a bird, suppose it spoke
the final words that fell
across its surface. Suppose
smoke had a memory.
Suppose it had a voice.
Suppose someone was listening,
someone with a pen and ink
and paper. Suppose there was
a list and that the clouds
could read it. Suppose they
broadcast it into space. Names
of stars. Names of birds. Names
called and no one answers.

2.

The trees drink up their fallen
leaves and burgeon forth in new-made
green each spring. But how shall the body

of humankind resorb its losses?
Gone each never-to-be-reconstructed face
and the labyrinth behind it. Gone
each sack of memory, the pet names
and nightmare imps. That razor-wire smile
of rage has been extinguished
and with it the eyes cutting back and forth.
The timbre of a voice is whirled away
into extinction, it will not be heard again,
nor will be seen a certain grace
in gliding in and out of chairs. The world

frays and frays. It pours
its riches out and out.

3.

Ghosts of strangers rush out of this world
like doors slamming and our hearts are
sucked into that void. But then ebb back. We cannot

sustain it, this tenderness for the unmet and
newly dead. Our mourning for such as these
is an ephemera. And so they languish

in some anteroom of grief, unattended.
They mill about, sip thin, terrible,
bitter coffee. And then set their cups

in saucers with a little clink, and turn
and go, seeing that we are faithless, no
use to them at all. Tatters of sorrow

blow after them. They do not turn to look.

4.
And if the day is dreary and smudged,
who will claim it?
If the hour is out at the elbows
and down in its heels,
who will stand up and take it home?
This tarnished minute,
this rusted week burning oil in blue smoke—
will anyone bid for it?
Time when nothing happens,
tedious time,
time with a headache
or an argument
or an unpaid bill past due
or the seconds just now passed—
who would miss them?
Ai Ai Ai
cry the voiceless dead reaching out
with their no hands.

Eileen Murphy

49 YEARS OLD
LAKELAND, FLORIDA

A long-time writer and poet, I recently moved from Chicago back to my native Florida. I live in a semirural area with my muse-pack: fellow writer Jeff, dog Mish, cat Lucky. We're surrounded by cow pastures and orange groves, and cultivate organic sweet potatoes, pole beans, tomatoes, strawberries, broccoli, lettuce, basil. From time to time, box turtles, finches, armadillos, rabbits, foxes, cranes, and mosquitoes call our property their home. I have published poetry, short stories, and book reviews in the Louisville Review, Mudfish, *the* Kerf, George & Mertie's Place, Lonzie's Fried Chicken, *the* Post-Amerikan, Black Dirt, Rhino, KotaPress, *and a number of other small press and on-line journals.*

APRÈS MOI LE DÉLUGE

When I heard about
the next World War
I stuck a stone in my backpack, a stolen star.

I tried to unplug
my electric sheep.
I stroked pink lipstick, I paid to cheat.

I baked in a bunker
buried in my dress
as hot birds flew bombs north by northwest.

I walked crooked streets
in my high heels,
I saw no other people for ten thousand miles.

I slept with an old sock,
I ate a moral pear.
In a dark car I was washing my hair

in ashes & Dove
when a dwarf knocked on the door
& said, "Have ya heard? We finally won the war."

———

Kevin Andrew Murphy

36 YEARS OLD
SAN JOSE, CALIFORNIA
Kevin Andrew Murphy is a science fiction and fantasy writer. His most recent credits are two novels, Fathom: The World Below *from iBooks and* Drum into Silence *from Tor.*

BAD FAIRIES

For Laura Bush, February 12, 2003.

Like fairies at a christening
the bad ones weren't invited
for fear of someone listening
to voices not united
in hymns of praise, yet glistening
with tears of rage they cited

the Belle's fair words, the grassy leaves,
the dreams that were deferred.

Like stormcrows gathered in the eaves
their echoed cries are heard.
Dark prophecies, each interweaves.
A single voice? Absurd.

———

Carol Muske-Dukes

57 YEARS OLD
LOS ANGELES, CALIFORNIA
Professor at the University of Southern California. Recipient of many awards including the Alice Fay Di Castagnola Award of the Poetry Society.

The House of Bush

This is the house of madness.

This is the man who sits in the house of madness.
This is the time of the man named Bush who sits in the house of madness.
This is a time-bomb ticking away in the time of the man named Bush who sits in the house of madness.

This is the child strapped to the bomb ticking away the time of the man named Bush who sits in the house of madness.
This is the ravaged land of the child strapped to the bomb ticking away
the time of the man named Bush who sits in the house of madness.

These are the years and the cries of loss, the starving poor,
the reeling stocks, the chanting young, the face of the child
strapped to the bomb ticking away the time of the man
  named Bush
          who sits in the house of madness.

These are the oil wells pumping dry, the corporate lies,
  the Enron ties,
the reeling stocks, the jobless lines, the face of the child
  strapped to the bomb ticking away by a cyclone fence
  with a nickel bag in Our Hometown
in the time of the man named Bush who sits in the
  house of madness.

These are the oil wells across the sea, the dictator's deal, the
torturer's cage, the affairs of state in the ravaged land of
  the child
strapped to the bomb ticking away in the time of the
  man named Bush who
          sits alone in the all-White House of madness.

Majid Naficy

51 YEARS OLD

SANTA MONICA, CALIFORNIA

Was politically active against Shah of Iran. Wife and brother assassinated during Revolution. Has published books: Muddy Shoes; Father and Son; In Search of Joy: A Critique of Male-Dominated, Death-Oriented Culture in Iran. *Ph.D. from UCLA.*

I Do Not Want You, Petroleum

I don't want you, petroleum!
For a long time,
I thought that you burnt for me.
Now I see that I am burning for you.

I'm not saying that it's not pleasant
Sitting near a kerosene heater
And enjoying the falling snow.
Or the working water pumps
In the empty plain.
And yet, I can not believe you,
Seven-headed dragon!
Fire still spews forth from your mouth
To the soul of my homeland.

In your school I learned servitude,
So that the Khan of the tribe
Could send his son to London,
The Imperial Army in Mohammara
Forced me to abandon
The dream of a "House of Justice."
On the street my blood was shed,

It turned into ink
For the pens which wrote
The new contracts of slavery.
The grand gates of falsehood
Opened with your keys.
Today the promised Messiah rides
On you, donkey of the Antichrist.

You raised this state to the heavenly throne
And polished its boots to a sheen.
You raised its seven-headed club
And whenever I tried to pull it down
You reinforced its shaky body
With your sturdy beams.
No! I don't want!
I don't want you, petroleum!
Oh, bloody stream!
For a long time,
I thought you gave me blood.
Now I see, you made me bleed.

———

Aruna Nair
17 YEARS OLD

Voices

The blank-solemn newsreader fades
to blurry faces, blurry placards
"Not in my name!" The exclamation
hangs in the air, overexcited, silly. Shrug.
Turn off the TV. And cast now cast
your mind back
five years four
maybe one or two
back to those blue
TV glares, the shimmering grin
of that man in the suit
Step out. Step out. Voice. Vote.
Make it count.
It was all
gloss and glimmer then
this joke that honest frown
the pale white glitter of a smile under cameras.
Mouthing your voice. And now
at this distant date
all that cast long ago, half vague
thinking then of tax and transport and slick-backed hair,
is turning, turning suddenly, water to the deepest red,
that voice to paper that vote to blood.

———

Marilyn Nelson
Poet Laureate of Connecticut.

Unrhymed Peace Sonnet

Who are the Good Guys now? Who are the bad?
Nobody's wearing Stetsons, black or white.
Each has a history of evil deeds:
one individual, one centuries
of rapine and ideals. It's almost noon.
One leader straps on bombs. The armies mass.
We'll blow that s.o.b. to kingdom come,
everyone thinks; bring on Armageddon!
Yosemite Sam, frustrated and enraged,
jumps up and down, shooting holes in the clouds.
And Africa is dying out, of AIDS.
Why the hell doesn't the moving finger write?
What the hell are you waiting for, my God?
Why don't you tell those bastards not to fight?
For Pete's sake, send an angel! Burn a bush!

Randolph Nesbitt

47 YEARS OLD
ALISO VIEJO, CALIFORNIA
closet poet/artist/photographer, mortgage broker by trade

War Haiku

tanks charred, black and silent
bodies sun-scorched, chemical-soaked
lizard flicks its tongue

———

Michelle Nolder

35 YEARS OLD
CALIFORNIA
An unpublished poet but a poet nonetheless...

Whose Wonderland Is This?

I want another cup of tea
Before I go on trial tonight
I stand accused of not loving my country
If I do not support its policy
As if the policy of this
Mad Hatter political occupation
Reflects the Wonderland I
Used to call America
Your Alice, your sweet Alice
Loves that Wonderland

But I'll grab that March Hare
And yell, "Can you be sure there is
No alternative?" in its face
As many times as my conscience requires . . .

My Cheshire Cat prosecutor
With a smug smile and agenda all his own
Tells me not supporting a war
Is the same thing
As not supporting our troops
But the last time I checked
I am the only one on this stand
Who has a loved
One on a ship scheduled to
Die on the ground
For something hidden
Somewhere underneath it
As if we don't have things hidden
In teapots scattered all over
This Homeland Security infested
Garden as they watch
What I type
What I buy
What I read
To see if I measure up to
What an "American" should be
According to the white rose
Red rose definition published
By whichever upgraded version of
McCarthy wields the pen
Paint those roses red boys
As many times as you need to

To convince us the
Capacity of atrocity
The newly installed King of Hearts
Can so easily commit
Is the proper thing to do
And what it is to be an American
Is to walk in step with the
Drums of spoons on cups

Apparently I'm guilty
The jurors voted using punch cards
(How ironic)
And the punishment is this
I get to eat the biscuit
That makes me smaller
While they get to eat the biscuits
That make them bigger
Than they have any right to be . . .

Leonard Nolt

54 YEARS OLD
BOISE, IDAHO USA

I've had poems, photographs, and articles published numerous times and have been active in peacemaking and environmental preservation efforts throughout my adult life, influenced largely by my Anabaptist heritage and by the examples of my friends and associates.

I Write This to Report . . .

I am now standing, with others, in
Acteal, Mexico, at the very place where,
on December 22, 1997, paramilitaries
massacred forty-five Christian pacifists,
thirty-six women and children, while
they worshipped, fasted, and prayed.

A soft wind curls around the coffee
and banana trees. Rain falls like the
tears of the bereaved, hesitating only a
second on the steep earth before
racing, as if in fear, toward the
sea. No birds sing.

Quietly we stand in the memorial
building, constructed on the graves of
the victims, gazing at photos of the
people who died. Their clear eyes return
our stare, awaiting an answer to the
unspoken question.

Soon night will cover this mountain
town, but nothing in this life will

cover the grief felt for the loss of Rosa
Vasquez Luna, Catarina Luna Perez,
Josefa Vazquez Perez, Maria Gomez
Perez, Margareta Mendez Paciencia,
and forty others who died that day.

While shadows of death brush our shoulders,
we circle and kneel, blowing gently on the
glowing embers of peace, watching,
as the flame begins to rise.

Michelle Noullet
Hanoi, Vietnam
Teaching in Asia since 1980, including ten years working in the Southeast Asian refugee camps, the result of the last US military involvement.

The Grace of Angels

Who combs her long black hair,
ties it so carefully at the nape
with bright scarlet bows?
You wonder this each day
as she comes into your class.
Her handless arms that end in
fleshy mounds could never maneuver
such intricate twists of ribbon.
You worry how she can remember
English words without writing them,
but she knows her lessons as well

as the rest, black eyes bright
with greeting each morning.
On another morning in her village,
bombs exploded, shrapnel splitting screams,
shredding bamboo and bones.
Who buttons her neatly pressed blouse,
puts the gold hoops through her ears,
snaps the clasp of the Buddha pendant,
dangling protection from her delicate neck?
Perhaps it is her mother,
who once holding a perfect infant,
watching tiny fists uncurl, then grasp
her own finger, never guessing her daughter
would walk one day with the grace of angels,
stumpy wings fluttering from her side.

—

William O'Daly

51 YEARS OLD
AUBURN, CALIFORNIA

I am a poet, novelist, essayist, and the translator of six volumes of the late and posthumous poetry of the Nobel laureate Pablo Neruda for Copper Canyon Press. I am also a co-founder of the press, and make my living as a teacher, editor, and instructional designer.

To the Forty-third President of the United States of America

Mr. President, our history speaks to us, the history of Chile
and China, El Salvador and Nicaragua, Somalia, Puerto Rico—
today, our solemn duty is to defy your willful aggression,
to parse provocative words and habits, your heroic battle
to distract us. Perhaps you think God will protect us
from the religious zealots who sanctify your rule,
from your opportunism and the race renewal,
the investiture you have assumed because, as
always, it is not yours. Let me ask
an obvious question.
                  If we are to establish peace
and security for our nation, must we not do
everything in our power to end
the beginnings of war, must we not allow
our imaginations to craft a lasting peace?
Are not the children you would choose
to incinerate our own? We try on masks
to trick our isolated, frightened selves,
to propagate our sacred uncertainties
among the children of this blue planet,
a world we create and ruin every day.

                    Mr. President,
where do we walk, where may we sit down,
where can we work or rest, weep or pray,
what field does a man sunder and seed
in a country living only in memory, dying
every day at the hands of those who profess
to love her most? They say God loves America,
and that this "old bitch gone in the teeth" is
heaven on earth; in preemptive violence,
in obstinacy, in entitlements for the rich,
this murdered land, this, the people's
earth, is our reward for being right
no matter how wrong we are.
                    What "urge and rage"
thrives in the American heart, that so many cheer
this obsessive, unilateral madness?
                    Even through
precise layers of glass, the TV peddling
a thrilling efficiency, we cannot see them,
the ghosts that inhabit our malnourished
statistics, inhospitable closets, cold kitchens
where we eat meat and raise goblets of wine
to celebrate our belief that they are not like us.
I want to spend more time with my daughter,
my five-year-old, I want to see her, to know
she is alive. It is her "evening of the morning,"
she is just fine, though she implores me to tell her
the "acommitation of naked truth."
                    I imagine
Iraqis, weakened by sanctions, spending time
with their children. What do they play together,
what makes them laugh, what crude medicine

do parents spoon down fevered throats, when
they too are roused from nightmares of fragile
necklaces of bone, slung around the necks of
American fighters whose hearts we camouflage?
Who will witness the small charred bodies floating
in the Tigris, children writhing in pain, in smoking rubble,
in the ruins of Bab al-Wastani or the Mirjan Mosque,
severed limbs and glazed eyes that last night
followed their favorite story by candlelight?
                    Mr. President,
what does it mean when you say Saddam Hussein,
Butcher of Baghdad, official liar, terrorizes himself?
If he brings terror upon himself, will our dark angels
exterminate him or his already wounded people;
and would you answer Mr. Korb: What if Kuwait grew
     carrots, what if Iraq's
main exports were chick peas and cotton shawls
destined for American women
longing for the exotic?
                    To be honest,
I have forgotten from what we must abstain,
yet we know how to prevent conception. *"C'est la vie,"*
you say, saddled up, ready to ride with your posse
across oil fields just like those in Texas.
It appears the one thing we cherish
more than petroleum or our children
is the greased machinery of destruction.

Notes

1. "old bitch gone in the teeth": Ezra Pound, from "Hugh
Selwyn Mauberley"

2. "urge and rage": Anne Frank, from *The Diary of a Young Girl* (1947; tr. 1952), entry for 3 May 1944

3. "evening of the morning": Kyra Gray O'Daly

4. "acommitation of naked truth": Kyra Gray O'Daly

5. Bab al-Wastani: the last remaining of the renowned gates of Baghdad

6. Mirjan Mosque: ancient mosque, completed in 1358

7. "If Kuwait grew carrots we wouldn't give a damn." Lawrence Korb, former U.S. assistant secretary of defense, on the motives for "Operation Desert Storm"

8. "The war on terror involves Saddam Hussein because of the nature of Saddam Hussein, the history of Saddam Hussein, and his willingness to terrorize himself." George W. Bush

9. "*C'est la vie*": "Either they are with us or not. Either one is fine. *C'est la vie.*" An aide to George W. Bush, quoting him

10. "I know some in Europe see me as a Texas cowboy with six-shooters at my side. But the truth is I prefer to ride with a posse." One senior Bush aide, recalling President Bush's comment to Czech President Vaclav Havel in Prague (Fall 2002)

Gregory Orr

Refusing

Refusing the invitation
I was not given,
being given instead
the invitation to refuse.
Which I accept.
Am grateful for.
The chance to be part of
the poets' chorus,
the caucus of those
whose politics
is obvious and earnest.
Whose wishes are simple:
sensible diplomacy,
everything to be negotiated.
Tough bargaining,
but easy on the violence.
That's what we poets
learned from poems:
it's all on the table,
but it's stupid
to break up the table
with an axe,
to splinter the chairs.

And it's madness
to ask poets to celebrate,
when people can't even
breathe deeply
for fear of war's imminence.

Simon Ortiz

Simon Ortiz was the 1993 recipient of a Lifetime Achievement Award from the Native Writer's Circle of America.

Dear Sam,

My prayers are with you. When the sun is shining, we must receive its wamth. When the wind blows, we must breathe the air. We must let life live, and we must live. We must live; there is no choice.

Love, your brother,

Simon

No Choice

There is no choice.
We must not kill life.
There is no choice.
We must let life live.
There is no choice.

We must live.
We must live.

Alicia Ostriker

65 years old
Cambridge, England (at present); usually Princeton,
New Jersy

Author of ten volumes of poetry, most recently The Volcano
Sequence. *Twice finalist for National Book Award. Mother of three,
grandmother of two, lover of language, hater of lies.*

Thistle

Thistle at meadow's edge
Stands tall so that its crowns,
Royally purple, rise
Above the yellow-browns.

While weedy grasses pipe
Popular tunes, engage
In gossip or exchange
Pollen, noblesse oblige

Is thistle work, who guard
The entire field from woe,
Gorgeously costumed, hair
And gloves exactly so,

Whose spiky thorns around
Their chins proclaim or sing,
Noli tangere, friend,
There's no intent to sting

Unless we must. You see,
By reputation led,

Their point. Uneasy stands
The noble thistle head,

Perhaps. Or is it pride
That stiffens the green stalks?
Can thistles dream of being
Predatory hawks?

O doves among the rocks,
Be gently warned, pro tem,
Thistles are splendid, but
We stay away from them.

———

Eric Pankey

Eric Pankey is the winner of the Walt Whitman First Book Award.

History

A hundred flint arrowheads, chipped, rain-
        washed, scattered through a meadow of
        ragweed and clover,
The flesh they ripped, the rib nicked, the
        shields of horsehide torn, all lost to the
        elements;
An ice-pierced daybreak through a mica screen
        and the first lute arrives in China from
        Persia;

The uses of ambergris are perfected; the
        lamb's blood dries above the doorway; a
        glacier calves an iceberg;
From the rock where a father offered up his
        son as sacrifice, the Prophet ascends into
        paradise;
The summer you step on a rusted nail, the
        willows green and bend to the river; the
        river floods;

Before nightfall, a body is bargained for,
        secreted away in a borrowed grave fashioned
        from a cave;
Again, walls and towers topple. And no
        language but grief is left in common. And
        grief no language at all.
There is no history, only fits and starts,
        laughter at the table, lovers asleep,
        slaughter, the forgetfulness,

And yet for three nights straight, nothing but
        starlight—Byzantine, quicksilver, an
        emanation of a past,
And tonight you have renamed the
        constellations after the mudras: The
        Gesture Beyond Mercy,
The Gesture for Warding Off Evil, The Gesture
        of Fearlessness, The Gift-Bestowing Gesture
        of Compassion. . .

Sherman Pearl

68 YEARS OLD
SANTA MONICA, CALIFORNIA
Co-founder of Los Angeles Poetry Festival, co-editor of CQ (California Quarterly), author of three published collections of poetry, winner of several major awards, including National Writers Union's 2002 poetry.

The Poem in Time of War

should wake the city shouting EXTRA! EXTRA!
then whisper the story behind the story
like a conspirator. It should be short, stirring
as the president's call to arms;
soft enough for a flag at half-mast;
strong enough to stiffen the bereaved;
spacious enough to serve as a body bag.

The poem should carry the news that men
die miserably for lack of. It is
a brief on behalf of the living, a paper megaphone
for the voices of the dead. It must be
the world's last will and testament, a listing
of what will be left. It steals from forebears:
Sassoon's doomed diary and Auden's call to love.

The poem would be a prescription for healing
but who could read such a scrawl? . . . or a bandage
over the wounds, except that blood
tends to obliterate words.
Maybe all the war poems could be sewn together
into a vast thick quilt we'd pull around
our shoulders; might warm us on nights like this.

Jim Pearson
76 YEARS OLD
COVINGTON, LOUISIANA.
usmc ww2 korea scientist retired

kunishi ridge 2nd bn. first marines

hair in the trees
the voice of women
in the wind
singing for the children

155 mm howitzer
finest artillery piece
in the world
tot-2 (fire for effect)

hair in the trees
the voice of women
in the wind
singing for the children

81mm heavy mortar
finest heavy mortar
in the world
4 increments (fire for effect)

hair in the trees
the voice of women
in the wind
singing for the children

f4u-5 corsair
finest close air support aircraft
in the world
drop coordinates 34-65 (roger that)

hair in the trees
the voice of women
in the wind
praying for the children

Joel Peckham

32 YEARS OLD
MILLEDGEVILLE, GEORGIA

Dr. Joel B. Peckham, Jr., is an assistant professor of English and composition at Georgia Military College. A scholar of American Literature and a creative writer, Joel has had reviews, scholarly articles, and poetry published in numerous journals throughout the United States and Canada. Nightwalking, his first full-length poetry collection, was published by Pecan Grove Press in 2001. He is also co-founding editor of the online literary journal Milkwood Review *and an associate editor for GCSU's national literary journal,* Arts & Letters. *He currently lives with his wife, poet Susan Atefat Peckham, and his two children in Milledgeville, Georgia.*

Asleep at the wheel

We must love each other or die—Auden

I'm driving home from Atlanta, down 441—an unlit
stretch of highway winding through lakes and fields,
and I am fighting sleep—on the radio
someone explains the reasons for attacking Iraq.

I think of the photographs on CNN—gaunt Afghanis,
Palestinians. Kids—staring out the bombed-out shells
of their bodies. Wide awake, too awake with hunger
and fear. As a boy I remember most the dark unblinking
glitter of the eyes of fish—a rich obsidian depth that reached
back and down like canyons off Rockland—gleaming
with moving water and the reflections of leaves,
of quahog shells, of bright stones and the caught
gleam of sunlight in a torn can—or the gaze of anyone
leaning over the hull so far he almost tumbles into
gravity, longing, the deadly bliss

of children. Like too small fish shaken from trawl-nets
at predawn, my sons, flicker in oncoming beams
and disappear-the darkness slides across them,
takes them, throws them back into light again. And again,

I'm holding the baby against me; his first illness and
I'm terrified, his skin kindles mine—a gull caught
in old netting. His flail and scream against a sinking
down, a falling out of the world. In the distance,

the town sleeps and dreams of small things, grasses bend
and rise again in river water the way the head of a young
    boy
strapped upright in a car will loll and jerk back, loll—
a rhythmic, sickly dance that's hard to look at, too fragile
and human-like eyelids fluttering on a field of white
and the deep rich blackness of irises wide in sleep. I bite
my lip. There are no shoulders, no medians. We are
so near, and hurtling by each other
at great speed.
        And what was the name again
of the desert saint who, starving, came upon a vision
of a lion feasting on his own leg. Or a lamb, or
the saint himself. I can't remember, but it seems
important now.

Peter Pereira

43 years old
Seattle, Washington

I am a family physician in Seattle, and I deal on a daily basis with Cambodians who survived the US-led carpet bombing and subsequent disintegration of their peaceful country a generation ago. A war with Iraq is similarly unconscionable, and will cause millions of innocent people to suffer. Below is a poem from my work with Cambodian holocaust survivors.

What Is Lost

> *. . . everywhere and always,*
> *go after that which is lost.*
> —Carolyn Forché, *Ourselves Or Nothing*

When she came across the border
she had no shoes—only one black
Cambodian skirt, a thin blouse, the long
scarf they used for everything: sleeping,
bathing, carrying food, wrapping
the bodies of the dead.

She no longer wants to say
what happened to her husband and brothers,
afraid if words bring them back,
along will come the soldiers.
What do I have, she asks,
to keep the nightmares away?

Next to her guttural vowels
and clipped consonants, my English
strikes a tin note. The interpreter

translates my advice, and I wonder
which sound was nerve, which
was heart, which grief.

I give her another pill to try.
Perhaps with this one
she will sleep well
tonight. A sleep untroubled
by dreams, by memory.

She listens politely, smiles
a thank you: her only English.

Yet as I watch her leave
I know her cure comes Tuesday afternoons—
when she joins the circle
of other Khmer women to sew.
Punctuating the fabric
with yellow thread, binding her remnants
into a piece that will hold.

———

Marge Piercy
Wellfleet, Massachusetts
Sixteen books of poetry, fifteen novels, book of essays, memoir, anthology, play.

Choices

Would you rather have health insurance
you can actually afford, or bomb Iraq?
Would you rather have enough inspectors
to keep your kids from getting poisoned
by bad hamburgers, or bomb Iraq?
Would you rather breathe clean air
and drink water free from pesticides
and upriver shit, or bomb Iraq?

We're the family in debt whose kids
need shoes and to go to the dentist
but we spend our cash on crack:
an explosion in our heads or many
on the TV, where's the bigger thrill?
It's money blowing up in those weird
green lights, money for safety,
money for schools and headstart.

Oh, we love fetuses now, we even
dote on embryos the size of needle
tips; but people, who needs them?
Collateral damage. Babies, kids,
goats and tabby cats, old women sewing
old men praying, they'll become smoke
and blow away like sandstorms
of the precious desert covering treasure.

Let's go conquer more oil and dirty
the air and choke our lungs till
our insides look like stinky residue
in an old dumpster. More dead
people is obviously what we need,
some of theirs, some of ours. After
they're dead a while, strip them
and it's hard to tell the difference.

———

Robert Pinsky
Robert Pinsky was Poet Laureate of the U.S. from 1997–2000.

Statement of Conscience

Dear Mrs. Bush,

Thank you for your invitation to the White House event
on February 12, "Poetry and the American Voice." I appre-
ciate the honor and I welcome recognition of poetry's vital
presence in our country.

However, to my regret, I must decline to attend.

In our current political situation I am unwilling to partici-
pate in a Washington event that invokes an "American voice"
in the singular.

Specifically, I mistrust the president's contention that we
must invade Iraq preemptively, in defiance of important

allies, and contrary to the processes of international law. He asks us to trust him that this extraordinary, violent and uncertain plan is in our interest.

Like many other ordinary Americans, I wish I could trust the president even though I oppose his policies. But he has not been trustworthy: for example, using deceptive, misleading arguments for his tax proposals, speaking as though that proposal would help "average" Americans— which is a trick. On the issue of affirmative action, he hedged while running for office; now he is trying to hinder a modest, sensible affirmative action plan at a great state university, the University of Michigan; he uses deceptive language like "quotas" and "preferences": more accurate for the way members of rich, powerful families enter private universities like Yale.

In these areas, closer to home for me than geopolitics, I know that the president has not been trustworthy, so I cannot trust him on the world stage. To participate in a poetry symposium that speaks of "the" American voice, in the house of authority I mistrust, on the verge of a questionable war, is impossible—the more so when I remember the candid, rebellious, individualistic voices of Dickinson, Whitman, Langston Hughes.

I salute your intentions, and I hope a time may come when we will again be able to honor such great ancestors, wholeheartedly, together, at the White House.

Sincerely,

Robert Pinsky

Judy Platz
61 YEARS OLD
WESTERN MOUNTAINS
I have written and taught poetry for thirty years. Was part of the Kent State poet group.

Markers

> *for Mort Krahling (1944–1998)*
> *brother Bill and poets everywhere*

The mystery is
that we are still here at all—
still beating our owl wings
under curved moon;
star-nose moles digging, digging
in the dark, toward light
bones, teeth, bits of hair to identify the others—
words left behind on pages for channel markers
in the deep ocean of soul;
our temporal homes that see us invisible
with pen and hand and paper to create
artifacts, for those yet who will search.

The journey unrelenting, absolute;
but look! Seed tendrils walk beside us
in damp darkness
toward the light, always toward the light.

Katha Pollitt

Katha Pollitt was awarded the National Book Critic's Circle Award for Antarctic Traveller. *She is a columnist for* The Nation.

Trying to Write a Poem Against the War

My daughter, who's as beautiful as the day,
hates politics: Face it, Ma,
they don't care what you think! All
passion, like Achilles,
she stalks off to her room,
to confide in her purple guitar and await
life's embassies. She's right,
of course: bombs will be hurled
at ordinary streets
and leaders look grave for the cameras,
and what good are more poems against war
the real subject of which
so often seems to be the poet's superior
moral sensitivities? I could
be mailing myself to the moon
or marrying a palm tree,
and yet what can we do
but offer what we have?
and so I spend
this cold gray glittering morning
trying to write a poem against war
that perhaps may please my daughter
who hates politics
and does not care much for poetry, either.

Minnie Bruce Pratt

After the Anti-War March

We had a different driver on the way home. I sat
on the seat behind her, folded, feet up like a baby,
curled like a silent tongue in the dark jaw of the bus
until she flung us through a sharp curve and I fell.
Then we talked, looking straight ahead, the road
like a blackboard, one chalk line down the middle.
She said, nah, she didn't need a break, she was good
to the end. Eighteen hours back to home when
she was done, though. Fayetteville, North Carolina,
a long ways from here. The math of a mileage marker
glowed green. Was Niagara Falls near Buffalo? She'd
like to take her little girl some day, too little now, won't
remember. The driver speaks her daughter's name,
and the syllables ring like bells. I say I lived in her town
once, after another war. The boys we knew came home
men cocked like guns, sometimes they went off and
blew their own heads, sometimes a woman's face.
Like last summer in Ft. Bragg, all those women dead.
She says, "One was my best friend." Husband shot her in
front of the children, boy and girl, six and eight. She calls
them every day, no matter where she is. They get very
upset if she doesn't call. Her voice breaks, her hands
correct the wheel, the bus pushes forward, erasing nothing.
There was a blue peace banner from her town today,
and we said stop the war, jobs instead, no more rich
men's factories, refineries, futures built on our broke bodies.
She said she couldn't go to the grave for a long time,
but she had some things to get right between them so
she stood there and spoke what was on her mind. Now

she takes the children to the grave, the little boy
he wants to go every week. She lightly touches and
turns the big steering wheel. Her hands spin
its huge circumference a few degrees here, then
there. She whirls it all the way around when she
needs to. Later I hear the crinkle of cellophane. She
is eating some peppermint candies to stay awake.

———

Bill Ransom

57 YEARS OLD
OLYMPIA, WASHINGTON
Most recent books: Learning the Ropes *(poetry, essays, short fiction);*
Jaguar *(a novel). I worked as a medic in El Salvador, Guatemala, and
Nicaragua in the 1980s.*

EAVESDROPPING ON AMERICA

Women in the next booth compare shades of makeup,
shapes of their boyfriends' penises, prices of haircuts,
bikinis and blouses. They snap their gum, chainsmoke
and wonder how much their men love them—a dress,
trip to Hawaii, a new used car? Wars trouble them less
than reliability of the pill, pimples, their waiter's tight
black pants. They've had more men than years. With
army clothes and ignorance in fashion, love takes its chances
here-a greenhorn smuggler sweating out roadblocks.
Outside, in the street, two rabbits nailed to a stop sign.
Where can love, that thin guerrilla, take a stand?

David Ray
TUSCAN, ARIZONA

David Ray was co-founder with Robert Bly of American Writers Against the Vietnam War. He is author of several books, including a forthcoming memoir, The Endless Search, *and* One Thousand Years: Poems About the Holocaust.

SANDHILL CRANES CIRCLING THEIR TARGETS

Wang Wei claimed they were far more impressive
by moonlight—but that is hard to believe,

for these high-flying cranes fill the winter sky
as they whirl around in great circles. But their beauty

does not lighten my heart, for I know that equal
numbers of bombers are heading out over the sea,

throwing fear with each shadow—terror for terror—
real or imagined. These wings are gentler,

and eyes are not so robotic as those of pilots.
High above us thousands of cranes whirl and glitter,

then disappear, invisible to hunters and hawks.
When the sun strikes, it is as if the sky is filled

with confetti, or the lights have gone on high above
skaters who swoop and glide in similar glissandos—

but on thicker ice than that of our nation's policies.
Our leader declares that the war will be swift and short,

a sure victory. He sounds like Alcibiades addressing
the Athenians, convincing them to set out in their triremes.

But if he would read Thucydides he might learn
how such missions end in disaster, then perhaps

trade fighters and stealth bombers for cranes.

Arizona, January, 2003

F. D. Reeve

The Man Who Loved Music (In memory of Junius Scales, 1920-2002)

The moon is down; dark clouds compound the sky;
fog lies across the fields like a stone wall.
The rabbits march through village lane and street
shouting "JUST SAY NO!" "NO AXIS OF OIL!"
while the foxes circle in their high mahogany halls
counting their coins and what they'll eat if they fail to
  wipe out the rabbits once and for all.

War after war, blood chokes the earth. Bitter wind drives
  up the valley;
the past is lost in snow. Brutalized, the rabbit warrens burn

by thousands, unmarked, uncounted and unmoored.
"Not us!" the birds cry in the cold as they vanish south.
"ALL POWER TO THE FOX COLLECTIVE!"—force
     over freedom, lies from a fox's mouth.

Out of the dark comes a gentle, musical voice:
"while ignorant small-souled politicians control
the power and bully the whole world into war,
no one of conscience can slip away from the call to lead
     us to justice, equality and peace." Half-forgotten like a
First War marching song,
          his ghost flares up as dawn comes on.

Carlos Reyes
PORTLAND, OREGON

We Are Waiting for Peace to Break Out

—for Marvin Simmons

We are waiting for peace to break out
We are waiting for flowers to bloom
We are waiting for the moon to come
from behind the black clouds of war
We are waiting for the light
We are waiting
and as we wait we sing songs of celebration
We are waiting
and as we wait we hold out our hands in love and friendship:

white hands extended in friendship to black hands
and brown and green hands of the earth
We are waiting
and while we wait we applaud those who have gone
    before us
preaching peace: all the Martin Luther Kings, all the
    Gandhi's . . .
We are waiting for peace to break out
and as we wait we dance: we dance with the cold east wind
with the creaking singing branches of giant firs
we dance with the devils
of dust and the angels of clouds
We are waiting
and as we wait we are learning the language
of burning roses and the sunflowers slowly turning
    toward the sun
We are waiting for peace to break out
and while we wait we are learning to listen
to cries for mercy and cries for help
though we may not know the language
We are learning to listen for the arrival of doves
We are waiting for peace to break out
and while we wait we are smiling at you
at all of you—at the you and the me in the mirror . . .
We are waiting for peace to break out
We are waiting for buds to pop though it is deep winter
We wait for peace as patiently as the drop of water
on the lips at the mouth of the fountain
We wait knowing the water of peace is cool and sweet
sure that the crystal drop will fall on the earth
in spite of any of man's evil actions—

Adrienne Rich

Adrienne Rich has received the Bollingen Prize, the Lamnan Lifetime Axhievement Award, and the American Academy of Poet's Wallace Stevens Award.

The School Among the Ruins

Beirut. Baghdad. Sarajevo. Bethlehem. Kabul. Not of course here.

1.
Teaching the first lesson and the last
—great falling light of summer will you last
longer than schooltime?

When children flow
in columns at the doors
BOYS GIRLS and the busy teachers

open or close high windows
with hooked poles drawing darkgreen shades

closets unlocked, locked
questions unasked, asked, when

love of the fresh impeccable
sharp-pencilled yes
order without cruelty

a street on earth neither heaven nor hell
busy with commerce and worship
young teachers walking to school

fresh bread and early-open foodstalls

2.
When the offensive rocks the sky when nightglare
misconstrues day and night when lived-in

rooms from the upper city
tumble cratering lower streets

cornices of olden ornament human debris
when fear vacuums out the streets

When the whole town flinches
blood on the undersole thickening to glass

Whoever crosses hunched knees bent a contested zone
knows why she does this suicidal thing

School's now in session day and night
children sleep
in the classrooms teachers rolled close

3.
How the good teacher loved
his school the students
the lunchroom with fresh sandwiches

lemonade and milk
the classroom glass cages
of moss and turtles
teaching responsibility

A morning breaks without bread or fresh-poured milk
parents or lesson-plans

diarrhea first question of the day
children shivering it's September
Second question: where is my mother?

4.
One: I don't know where your mother
is Two: I don't know
why they are trying to hurt us
Three: or the latitude and longitude
of their hatred Four: I don't know if we
hate them as much I think there's more toilet paper
in the supply closet I'm going to break it open

Today this is your lesson:
write as clearly as you can
your name home street and number
down on this page
No you can't go home yet
but you aren't lost
this is our school

I'm not sure what we'll eat
we'll look for healthy roots and greens
searching for water though the pipes are broken

5.
There's a young cat sticking
her head through window bars
she's hungry like us

but can feed on mice
her bronze erupting fur
speaks of a life already wild

her golden eyes
don't give quarter She'll teach us Let's call her
Sister
when we get milk we'll give her some

6.
I've told you, let's try to sleep in this funny camp
All night pitiless pilotless things go shrieking
above us to somewhere

Don't let your faces turn to stone
Don't stop asking me why
Let's pay attention to our cat she needs us

Maybe tomorrow the bakers can fix their ovens

7.
"We sang them to naps told stories made
shadow-animals with our hands

washed human debris off boots and coats
sat learning by heart the names
some were too young to write
some had forgotten how"

James Rioux

33 YEARS OLD
EXETER, NEW HAMPSHIRE
My work has appeared in a variety of publications, including Prairie
Schooner, Five Points, *and* The North American Review.

February 2003—A sonnet

Old scripts and the dull eyes of cowboy scribes.
Winter rattles window panes and we can hear,
almost, the bombs and the "awe" they inspire,
the muted voices careening
down darkened corridors, the bloodthrob
buried in dust . . . Courage requires
vulnerability, the self flown
fully human in the chill and windwhip.
Upon whose altar does America
offer its flayed reason, its heart flung
withered and smoking onto the future's
cool stone tablature? And what God
will it turn its eyes to when night comes,
our dumbstruck pasts hung broadcast and shining?

Doren Robbins

53 years old
Los Angeles and Palo Alto, California

Doren Robbins' poetry has appeared in over fifty literary journals, including The American Poetry Review, North Dakota Quarterly, Cimarron Review, Indiana Review, International Poetry, Hawaii Review, Paterson Literary Review, Sulfur, New Letters, 5 a.m., Exquisite Corpse, Willow Springs *and* Hayden's Ferry Review.

NATURAL HISTORY

Tried to lift a swallowtail butterfly out
of a thick web, out of leg and wing fragments.
I think they were parts of moths and flies.
All the truncations, all the leaf chips,
dirty gauze strands, Chinese silver ash spores.
Held my thumb knuckle out for it to walk on.
That hesitating, that erotic clinging, that
flexing and trembling. At a garage window.
I forgot my tools inside the truck,
my work shoes by the pedals.
It came out on one thread. The window
behind the web was blank. Leather
insoles held the stained shapes of
my feet, those white swallows
pointing their beaks
at the underworld, pointing
at the carnivorous, pointing
and clinging. I was trying to lift it
through the leg and wing fragments
past the dry torso of a wasp.
Wrist bones secured with wire
in documentaries, fragmented in

my head. Mass grave photojournalism,
as usual quotas waiting for us,
incidental naturalism of our malice
documentaries went through my
interior gauze and webs. I was trying
to be steady. My hand close to the foot
below the wing, close to the breath
jumping on the rim of dirty strands.
To the antennae that looked moist,
to the remarkable fetal expression,
I held out my thumb knuckle.

———

Jessica Roeder

36 YEARS OLD
DULUTH, MINNESOTA
Born in Chicago during Vietnam War. Poems published in American
Poetry Review, Denver Quarterly, Nimrod. *Fiction in* Pushcart
Prize, Threepenny Review, Alaska Quarterly Review, *and others.*

A Plea

We ask of the birds only that they should bear us up. We
want to live and die among them. This is the way of my
untitled people. We have not been a people for long.

N——is the unspoken, unwritten name we give to where
we require to be now. We are humble. Yet our faith has
made us willing to be taken up on wings.

I met a nuthatch who had assumed the guise of a very old lady. She was the sort in the old days we would call a hag. Over the years her habitual shawl had shrunk to the size and negligibility of a headscarf. Density, too, volumes of lint, it had lost. The headscarf, even so, she clutched with accustomed vehemence. She would deputize no casual knot, no brooch to hold it. Dread to see the skin that hung at her neck.

Clever nuthatch, two-footed hopper. On her own, the old lady no longer moved. Every detail of her fall from fertility was a part of her disguise.

The birds send missionaries—clutchers, scatterers, pickers at crumbs—and though my people respond, we have no assurance that to their treetops they have yet lofted even one of us.

I would play tapes of their voices in the empty weekend city, where the pigeons and the falcon learn enmity again. Not a pigeon can bear us up, still less a falcon. Rather I, wearing red at all hours, will stand to be pierced again and again by the beaks of the hummingbirds. This is a rite of preparation. Where birds are, more substantial birds needs must appear.

Circle of the n——, circle of the bird eye, circle of pupil and iris, circle of the circle of the land around me, circle of the current, words, circle of beak wound, tree year, sky: I invoke you.

We are waiting for the sky to touch us. We are peaceful. We are losing our harsh, once echoing voices.

All we ask is that now, and again now, it should so begin.

Jerome Rothenberg

71 YEARS OLD
Encinitas, California

Jerome Rothenberg is an internationally known poet with over seventy books of poetry and several anthologies of traditional and contemporary poetry.

Statement of Conscience

In recent days, as part of the attempt to sanitize and justify the movement into war, we were treated to the following news from the United Nations: "The 'Guernica' work by Pablo Picasso at the entrance of the Security Council of the United Nations has been covered with a curtain. The reason for covering this work is that this is the place where diplomats make statements to the press and have this work as the background. The Picasso work features the horrors of war. On January 27 a large blue curtain was placed to cover the work."

Picasso, who was also a poet, wrote bitterly about the first horrors of aerial bombardment during the Spanish Civil War, but also about its continuation in the Second World War and after. For myself, working recently on translations of Picasso's wartime poems, I was hit by a sense of immediacy, first to feelings about Osama bin Laden's "blessèd terror" and then to George W. Bush and others hiding the truth behind blue curtains and "collateral damage" euphemisms while planning a new and greater air war.

The following, changed only in its title, will never reach the White House, but it may reach some others, in whom there is still a sense of resistance and hope.

The Dream & Lie of George W. Bush
(after Picasso's Dream & Lie of Franco)

that death could fall
from heaven on so many,
right in the middle of
rushed life
　　　　—Picasso, 1967

owl fandango escabeche swords of octopus of evil omen
furry dishrag scalps afoot in middle of the skillet bare
balls popped into a cone of codfish sherbet fried in
scabies of his oxen heart—mouth full of marmalade of
bedbugs of his words—silver bells & cockle shells & guts
braided in a row—a pinky in erection not a grape & not
a fig—commedia del l'arte of bad weaving & smudged
clouds—cosmetics of a garbage truck—the rape of las
meninas cries & outcries—casket on shoulders
crammed with sausages & mouths—rage that contorts
the drawing of a shadow that lashes teeth nailed into
sand the horse ripped open top to bottom in the sun
which reads it for the flies who tack a rocket of white
lilies to the knots spliced in the sardine heavy nets—
lamp of lice where dog is & a knot of rats & hide outs
in a palace of old rags—the banners frying in the skillet
twist in black of ink sauce spilled in drops of blood that
gun him down—the street soars to the clouds its feet
bound to a sea of wax that makes its guts rot & the veil
that covers it is singing dancing mad with sorrow—a
flight of fishing poles *alhigui* and *alhigui* of the moving
van first class interment —broken wings spinning in the
spider web of dry bread & clear water a paella made of
sugar & of velvet that paints a whiplash on its cheeks—

the light blocked out the eyes before the mirror that make monkeyshines the chunk of nougat in the flames that gnaws itself the lips around the wound—cries of children cries of women cries of birds cries of flowers cries of wood & stone cries of bricks cries of furniture of beds of chairs of curtains of casseroles of cats & papers cries of smells that claw themselves of smoke that gnaws the neck of cries that boil in cauldron & the rain of birds that floods the sea that eats into the bone & breaks the teeth biting the cotton that the sun wipes on its plate that bourse & bank hide in the footprint left imbedded in the rock.

———

Ruth Irupe Sanabria

27 YEARS OLD
PERTH AMBOY, NEW JERSEY

10

1.
Walking off the subway up the ramp through the turnstile
up the steps to the street—
I inhale

I am relieved today does not stink like September the
wind hardly moves—
the smell

Each day I walk onto W. 4th I hold my breath rejecting
the stench of fire

Today it is warm, there is no odor, maybe winter will be
gentle

2.
Regardless of season
Killing is never mild

3.
When the President of the University publicly proclaimed—
we were genetically defective, we learned our history quick

We looked to ancestors and took sides

Three years later I see you again
Taped to a wall
"Javier my son, he wear class ring"

4.
When the President of the United States publicly pro-
claimed war, I thought of all the homeland terror and
genocide that went into making us immigrants into
making us racially, all the homeland terror and genocide
that didn't want you to wear a class ring historically and
as we speak and at all costs and by any means and I
knew you would have opposed this particularly particu-
larly if waged in your name.

5.
today it is bright yellow
like spring or fall beginning

a bridge between spring and snow

you one of the thousands upon thousands
remind me how fragile passing time is

6.
urgent need
to talk
panic
to touch
you alive

I cannot rest
there is blood everywhere

7.
The pigeons in New York are missing pieces of themselves—
What's going on? They walk urgently
Between human feet. I have never seen humans
Fly, we are afraid of airplanes we are afraid of heights.

8.
The pigeons in Seattle are lean and glide
With grace alongside the gulls
Perhaps the fish and fruit and ample sky
Keep them healthy

They trust too much and sometimes
We throw alka-seltzer in the air
And watch them gracefully swoop
Down to catch our offerings

With their best pirouette and we watch
Them fly away until they explode inside
And crash like rocks onto the sidewalk

9.
the pigeons in D.C. are different
in Mt. Pleasant there is a park
we call El Parque de las Ratas

first people
then the rats then the pigeons
eat the trash

sometimes crossing El Parque
my sister and I would be hungry
I would say I know what we can do
let's kill that pigeon and eat it.
sometimes she was too hungry to laugh.

10.
to be honest with you I don't care how pigeons live or
    think I'm really thinking how paloma means pigeon
    and paloma means dove
how dove symbolizes peace but pigeon is a ubiquitous
    element of the human landscape and how the two
    meanings are not synonymous
in this language

Alexandra Indira Sanyal

8 YEARS OLD
CAMBRIDGE, MASSACHUSETTS

Alexandra is in the second grade in Cambridge, Massachusetts. She wrote this poem on February 7, 2003, a day when she was home sick from school and saw thirteen unexpected inches of snow falling in less than 8 hours outside the window at her home. Her class had written letters to President Bush a few days before composing this poem.

Untitled

Snow so fluffy and soft.
I like to run and jump into it.
It leads to peace and love.
Snow stops war
and fights
that lead to killing.
So snow come today.

Peggy Sapphire
64 YEARS OLD
CRAFTSBURY, VERMONT
Poetry has appeared in various journals, anthologized in several collections, former editor of Connecticut River Review, *a national poetry journal.*

The Presence of Justice

The simplicity is this,
the sage has told us:
". . . peace is not
the absence of war,
peace is
the presence of justice . . ."

It is the health of all our children,
none left to the bowels of an ER, last in
the line of the uninsured.
It is the thriving work life
of the able-bodied, the able minded,
the willing, the hard-driving, the
courageously striving.
It is the fair wage,
the medical care
the clean air.
It is the vote counted
when we pull the lever or
write a name.
It is our voices heard
singing ideas of hope,
when we are marching,

believing the power of people
to bring light
against the dark minds
of war-makers and profiteers.
It is along the longer road of wisdom
where peace is found.

———

Elizabeth Scanlon

Elizabeth Scanlon is an Associate Editor at The American Poetry
Review.

We Guide, We Follow

Like the blind for their seeing-eyes,
I have tenderness for you, my owed & owing
& would not see you harmed—
if not for your own good
then for mine.

———

Grace Schulman

Grace Schulman is the recipient of many awards including two Pushcart Prizes, and the Aiken Taylor Award for Modern American Poetry.

Statement of Conscience

Who harms his brother harms himself. Who sets his family's house on fire is himself consumed in flames. Protect our innocent Iraqi civilians. Honor their houses. Save them, our spirit, our kin.

The Journey Home

For Sam Hamill

It never changes: When bright arrows sang
like birds above the Yangtze, Tu Fu fled
past yellow autumn leaves, and past the scars
war wagons made in earth. Three years later,
he trekked back. Life away had been no life,
nor was there any forest or rock hollow
in which to hide. Now, peach and willow
                blooming,
he sipped rice wine, knowing there was no peace

I left my city once to where geese, black
against white skies, became flight squadrons,
juniper berries fallen in clumps on slate
scattered like nails, a cardinal's flight
stitched leaves with scarlet thread, color of
                blood.

A heron's wings were folded bandages.
Back to the flares of war, I ask for one
more day to praise brick buildings and white
                    pines.

———

Rebecca Seiferle

Not a War Song

Why should I, searching the thesaurus
for synonyms for "chant" and "cadence,"
try to make various and alive the unremitting
noise of war? Army cadence, battle chant,
if the behavior's unique to our species,
each bird or whale or wolf in solitary
call (though I'm not sure that I believe
this when all the wolves my neighbor owns
start howling to a police siren), the words of war
are as dull as the armor of the ruthless
Diomedes who stalked the goddess of love
to drive her from what had been the fields
and green pastures of Troy, now decimated
to an excremental slab of mud and limbs.
He pierced her veil of stars and fog to slash
her hand where bone meets palm. So war
is dependent for its reason and its myth
upon anecdotes of wounding someone's
lovely form, and the poet must be a solitary

singer (not necessarily nightingale, perhaps
common wren or western meadowlark,
its voice tightening across the distance),
singing a bleak and awkward beauty against
the commonality of war.

———

Matthew Shenoda
SAN FRANCISCO, CALIFORNIA

Enough

"The blood of the dead is not negotiable!"
Chilean Protesters in opposition of General Pinochet

It's happening again

It never stopped

I am living in the war that each of my ancestors died for

I am living in the bomb marked "revenge" whose steel
   will burst on the
necks of my brethren
whose toxins will leak into the water of my children's thirst

how many years must our children watch
the building of caskets, the withering of leaves
by graveside, by tombstone, by the rotting corpse
of their peers?

I am flying in the plane whose destruction can only be
    seen in infrared
whose image of humanity is a radar screen

we are a sharp edged machine
moving for your table
the axe of my tongue is oiled
its muscles tense for striking

I am living in the rifle adorned with stickers from
    sixteen-year old soldiers
who try and pretend that this life is normal

our trees are fed by the blood of our sisters
our fruit is sour, our soil is rich
our children wail shards of glass
our youth wear guns for shoes

I am an angry mob whose rage is fueled by falling stocks
who does not have time to care for the hungry, the
    disheveled or the
dead

hear my voice
my brother has ripped his heart from deep
beneath his ribs and left it on your plate

you have not seen freedom—the eyes
of the dead lurk inside your hollow skull

I am living in the tent of Palestinian children who wake
   each morning to
stand in the line marked "displacement"
who speak a language that is not enough

the blood of the dead is not negotiable
the wine of the wicked not sweet

I am living in the land of a regime that calls itself a
   nation under God
that shows no respect for creation

the blood of the dead is not negotiable
the wine of the wicked not sweet

I am living in Babylon somewhere between New York
   and L.A.

the blood of the dead is not negotiable
the wine of the wicked not sweet

I am living in the repetition of hysteria, a misanthropic
   record that spins
over and over on a player so broke no one can stop it

the blood of the dead is not negotiable
the wine of the wicked not sweet

I am living in a lake of tears that knows no border
a place where the salt is abundant and the water nonexistent

the blood of the dead is not negotiable
the wine of the wicked not sweet

I am living in America in this place that has spit on
everything I know to love

———

Gary Short

Statement of Conscience

I've been living in Guatemala for most of the past year,
and my Guatemalteco friends are puzzled by the desire of
this administration to engage in war with Iraq. They
believe that such action will only raise the level of hatred
in the world and increase, not decrease, the threat of
terror. They think that the impending actions of the U.S.
will make the world a more dangerous place. I agree with
them.

The idea of firing "peacekeeper missiles" and bombing
Baghdad in the name of peace, sickens me. How much
"collateral damage," in other more truthful words, how
many innocent children, women, elderly will die as a
result of a barrage of our killer missiles?

Both poets and political leaders should take care with
language and the use of the American voice. We ask our

political leaders to take care and urge restraint with our use of American force.

American Light

I watched the distant explosions.
The bursting bombs struck matches
in the night, brief flares
beyond the bedroom window. Who's there?
My mother said it wasn't anything—
a practice bombing on the Bravo Range,
just think of fireworks
on the 4th of July.

I leaned against the cold window,
closed my eyes to a deeper night.
The distant white flashes & the rumble
like a panicked horse running.
Across the hall I could hear my mother
fuss at her hair in the mirror.
She'd put on lipstick & her blue dress
to wait for my father's return from the bar.

Five miles away in town, two searchlights
from the Ford dealership
cut the black sky into angles.
On the highway out of town, burning beyond
my sight & understanding, a red-neon
pulsing whorehouse heart beckoned
bomber crews from the air force base.

My mother waited, looked out on the long dirt road
for roving headlights to show

among the crowd of lights, seen & unseen.
When the bombing stopped, the stars
seemed brighter, more quiet.
Falling asleep I might have dreamed
the future—Baghdad on fire,

or a Vietnamese girl trying to outrun
her own burning skin.
My mother told me to sleep tight,
not to be afraid.
Where she kissed me good-night,
lipstick flamed red on my cheek.

———

Jim Shugrue

54 YEARS OLD
PORTLAND, OREGON
Jim Shugrue lives, writes, and works as a bookseller in Portland.

On A Photograph of a Severed Hand

What is the sound of one hand
lying in the middle of a road
waving goodbye to its lost body?

How has it come this far from a hand
to mouth existence? How did it earn
its crust of callus? Is this

the right hand or the left? I cannot
tell. This is a photograph of a hand;
they could print it either way.

I've never seen a hand, alone,
open and empty in the middle
of a road, and pray to the god

they tell me has us all
in his good hands never to see one.
I know what history is. Our hand—

me—down bodies are mostly water,
and we spend them in tears and sweat.
Here is my hand. Take it,

and give me yours, while we
are still attached.

W. D. Snodgrass
77 YEARS OLD
SAN MIGUEL DE ALLENDE, MEXICO
Pulitzer Prize in Poetry, 1960.

Statement of Conscience

I am in Mexico and only now learned of the anti-war web-site and your campaign of poets against Bush's planned attack on Iraq. I congratulate you on this action. It is of prime importance that we do everything we can to counter plans which would make us guilty of the kind of aggression we once condemned when undertaken by the Fascists or Communists. Such acts would be truly un-American. Though it may appear that the Bush forces are winning their war against the poor in the U.S., there is no reason to start slaughtering the inhabitants of other countries which are already starving. Hatred of America is spreading: why throw Iraq's oil onto those brush fires?

Every success to you,
W. D. Snodgrass

Primus St. John

63 YEARS OLD
WEST LINN, OREGON

Primus St. John was born in New York City and raised by West Indian grandparents. One of five artists who inaugurated the NEA's Poets in the Schools program, St. John is the recipient of an Oregon Book Award and a Western States Book Award, received nominations for the American Book Award and the PEN West USA Award, and has taught literature and creative writing at Portland State University for the past thirty years.

If There Were No Days, Where Would We Live (excerpt)

The heart line begins
on the thumbless side of the palm
traveling horizontally under the fingers,
when it is clear & deeply etched
you have deep emotions...
so the war is over, my love,
and we have killed enough of them,
torched their homes
trampled their fields
mutilated their arms
burned their legs
harvested their ears
and wore them like dark pearls
drove them crazy
made night a sure sign
of death
their schools, lost canyons
with nothing blowing through them

and an exact count of
dead mothers
dead fathers
dead children
and all that was given
taken away.
What do you do now
with the hunger
and the poverty glaring in their faces?
St. Teresa
would have probably kissed it,
but we were not saints
we were soldiers
hiding in the enemy's world.
How many times
must I be dipped into the water
to be a child again?

———

John L. Stanizzi
CONNECTICUT

CHILDREN PLAYING—after the Persian Gulf War

The heavy equipment,
done for the day,
is parked here and there
on the stripped lot,
among hills of dirt
and felled trees,
scattered lumber
and half-framed houses.
Seven children are walking there,
single file,
their studied silhouette
as exact and crisp
as if it had been precisely cut
from the newspaper;
the familiar, sad gait;
the hands on top
of bowed heads;
the last child
pressing a plastic machine gun
to the lower back
of the child in front of him
walking there in the dusk,
playing surrender,
April exploding everywhere.

Don Stanley

85 years old
Westlake Village, California

A staff announcer for the NBC television network for forty-six years. This poem was written late one night in 1944 as I lay in a bunk at boot camp—a young man waiting to be sent to another war.

Untitled

Weep not, oh world, for these, your valiant slain,
For bodies sodden with the fallen rain,
Weep not for those who died.
There was no heartbreak there,
But rather weep for those who yet must stay,
Whose battle is not done, nor this the end,
Who gladly at that moment would have said,
"Let it be me instead,"
Yes, weep for these.

Yes, weep for her who in that distant day,
Bore pain with pleasure, fear with fervent hope,
Who gently kissed the childish fear away,
Who planted love so deep within the seed
And saw the fruit lay fallen from the tree.
Yes, weep for her.

And weep for her who gave another love
A love of youth and laughter in the sun,
Of lips that gave the weary body rest,
And eyes that gave the flagging soul its peace.
A deep, consuming fire in the night
That now is ashes in an empty tomb,

Whose heartbeat is an empty clatter in an empty room.
Yes, weep for her.

And weep, oh world, your bitterest tears of all
For these, whose world should know no rancor yet,
Whose fairy tales should still be sweet and bright,
Who should not waken crying in the night
For someone who could make all troubles right
But does not come.
The cinnamon bear and rocking horse
No longer want to play
And evening prayers remain
Unanswered through the day.
Oh weep for these.

Yes, weep for all of these, oh world,
For victor, vanquished, friend and foe alike
For these thy children whose hands and hearts do bleed
Whose fears and sorrows go beyond the need
Weep till your tears have washed away your greed
Weep, weep, oh world . . . oh weep for these.

Ruth Stone

VERMONT

Ruth Stone is a winner of the National Book Award. She is 87 years old.

Be Serious

Perhaps it will snow.

Oh do be serious.

We know that Washington is thick in bunting

and Bush posters.

A crow of sadness

for the myth of democracy.

A Supreme Court appointed head of government,

a Republican Supreme Court appointed Republican
president.

But what's a president?

And what is democracy?

Now we can see how

all those other countries

and states

and republics

live under their tyrants.

How the poor die in the streets.

Karen Swenson

we

In a museum of the city
once called Saigon, are snapshots. One's
been blown up so we can all see
it clearly. An American,

a young foot soldier, stands on battle
pocked land, his helmet at a jaunty
tilt, posed for buddies as the Model
Grunt. In his left hand he is dangling,

like Perseus, a head by its hair.
Though not Medusa's, it's his charm
for turning fear to stone. Its stare
will quiet, awhile, his throbbing chest.

The tattered flesh that once dressed collar
bones hangs rags from this Vietnamese
neck, captured with the soldier's scar
of grin by a friend's camera.

Is it enough to see it clearly?
We all know what to think. The whitewashed
walls of a second room show nearly
as many black-and-white shots of

Cambodian atrocities
against Vietnamese. No room's hung
with what was done to enemies
of Vietnam, just as there's no

American museum built
to show off snapshots of My Lai.
One pronoun keeps at bay our guilt
they they they they they they

—

Arthur Sze

The Aphrodisiac

"Power is my aphrodisiac."
Power enables him to
connect a candle-lit dinner
to the landing on the moon.
He sees a plot in the acid
content of American soil,
malice in the configuration
of palm-leaf shadows.
He is obsessed with
the appearance of democracy
in a terrorized nation.
If the price of oil
is an owl claw, a nuclear
reactor is a rattlesnake
fang. He has no use
for the song of an oriole,
bright yellow wings.
He refuses to consider
a woman in a wheelchair

touching the shadow of
a sparrow, a campesino
dreaming of spring.
He revels in the instant
before a grenade explodes.

———

Paula Tatarunis
51 YEARS OLD
WALTHAM, MASSACHUSETTS

Guernica Pantoum

Of the eighteen eyes in Guernica, sixteen are open.
Of its nine mouths, eight gape and cry.
There is a bull, a bird, a horse, one child broken,
one mother grieving; elsewhere, others fall, flee, watch, die.

Not nine mouths, but eight gape and cry
with impeccable lips, palates, tongues, teeth.
One woman grieves; others fall, flee, watch, or die
while lance and flame menace their raw breath.

With impeccable lips, palates, tongues and teeth
eight mouths siren terrible laments
until lance and flame, transfixing their raw breath,
become the pivot of a deathward dance.

Eight mouths will siren terrible laments
for a child's face folded like a sleeping rose.

Around the pivot of a deathward dance
sixteen eyes glare like embers, cannot close.

I sing for a child's face, a sleeping rose,
beside a bull, a bird's throat, a pierced mare,
under sixteen eyes like embers that refuse to close
amidst fanged flames and cascades of hair;

I sing for a bull, a bird, a pierced mare
as darkness and dust refract gray arcs-en-ciel
collapsing between fanged flames and falling hair,
between candlewicks and the ghosts of petals.

As darkness and dust refract gray arcs-en-ciel
savagery inspects, approves what it has fractured.
Between candlewicks and the ghosts of petals,
it celebrates what it has tainted and ruptured.

Savagery extracts the joy from what it's fractured
then spills and wastes it on the hungry dust.
It celebrates taint amidst the strew and rupture
beneath an icy sun and incendiary frost.

Spilled and wasted on the hungry dust,
joy will take root and rise as rage,
and thrive on icy sun or incendiary frost,
then march like soldiers off the burning page.

Spilled joy will take root and rise as rage,
will speak for the lips that have fallen together
will charge like armies off the bitter page
will riot like paint beyond the frame's tether.

They call us from the ruins—four weeping women,
a bull, a bird, a horse (one woman and one child
   broken.
Of what they have seen let us sing and sing again!
(Of the eighteen eyes in Guernica, sixteen are open.)

Terry Tempest Williams

Freedom From Speech

The erosion of voice is the build up of war.
Silence no longer supports prayers,
but lives inside the open mouths of the dead.

February 12, 2003.

Karma Tenzing Wangchuk

56 YEARS OLD
APOLLONIA, SIFNOS, GREECE
*Lay Buddhist monk and poet, former president of PEN New Mexico.
This poem was first published in RAW NerVZ, Canada.*

none. a tanka

After the rain,
she finds puddles
to jump in—
my child, knowing nothing
of the storms to come.

Elaine Terranova

Choral Song

foreseeing the Trojan War, from Euripides' Iphigenia at Aulis,
tr. Elaine Terranova

Soon Greek oars will whip up
silver eddies in the Simois,
and Troy's flashing river
will carry our fleet in battle gear
into the sun-drenched plains Apollo rules.
I see Cassandra shaking out
her wild yellow hair.

Her head is wreathed in laurel,
a sign the prophecy
is moving through her. And though
the god's breath fills her words,
no one will hear. From the tops
of their towers, armed Trojans
stare out toward the sea.
Even so, the war god will sail past,
invisible, leading battleships
and the onslaught of spears and arrows.
He is on his way to Priam's hall
to greet the one who's hiding there,
Helen, Zeus' child, seed of blood and tears.

Her brothers, the Dioscuri,
shine like stars in heaven.
She is herself the light of battle.
Then Ares will bring the war
to Pergamos, the holy place of Troy,
circling it in blood. He will build
a wall of corpses, thick as stone.
Throats will be cut, heads severed
from bodies. Then from the citadel
to the meanest hovel
he will sack the city,
bleed from each dwelling place
all it has to offer.
He will leave the women keening,
and with them Priam's queen.
Even Helen will cry out,
who long ago deserted
home and husband for this place.

O women of Chalcis,
let us remain guiltless,
my own children and theirs
never cross the will of heaven,
never call down such wrath
on our land. Let none of us
know a day so sunless,
for now the shadow of doom
is falling over those Lydian ladies.
And in that darkness, even the gold
wound around their necks
no longer shines. Their weaving
put aside, they will call out
in fear to one another,
"Who has come to seize me by the hair,
tearing me out of my native earth
as easily as one plucks a flower?"

Holly Thomas
46 YEARS OLD
SEATTLE, WASHINGTON

Chiapas

I don't know you, child.
I've never seen your country
or spoken your tongue.
But I see you burning
like an oil-soaked rag
in one of the old farm trucks
torched to terrify your people,
burning alone
because you fell asleep
after a long day's bending
in stone fields,
too tired at day's end
to walk back home.
Or, because you were
dragged there
conscious, and
set aflame.

Your mother devours your murderers' hearts
in her drugged dreams.
Your father, "disappeared" after the burning,
eats his own.

William Irwin Thompson

64 YEARS OLD
CAMBRIDGE, MASSACHUSETTS
Author of sixteen books; semi-finalist National Book Award, 1972; Oslo Poetry Festival Award, 1986. Founder of the Lindisfarne Association.

Cambridge Rant

Dear Mr. President,

When first did standing up before a crowd
crowd out the truth? When first did Americans
become consenting addicts to deceit?
Did it start with FDR's feigned surprise
in his famous day in infamy's speech,
or back with Wilson's "war to end all wars"?
Or did it begin with our own sinking
the Maine and blaming it on the Cubans
so that the American Empire could
set its ramparts out from Puerto Rico
to Hawaii and the Spanish Philippines?
Or should I go farther back to Lincoln
"the Great Emancipator" who did not
want to free the slaves but only ship
the inferiors back to Africa?
Honest Abe was our first Imperial
Bismark suspending habeas corpus,
to forge the industrial nation-state
and cover death with his own deathless prose.
Or, President Bush, should we date it back
to the Mexican-American War?
A few Gulf of Tonkin lies are buried there.

Let's stop before we go too far and end
with duplicitous Thomas Jefferson.
To save the myth of our Founding Fathers,
let's stop with populist Andrew Jackson—
the Charlton Heston hero on a horse—
a sharp real estate speculator
who hated Indians to get their lands,
a real leader of men who ordered
execution for an adolescent
who when swamp-soaked and mosquito-bitten
was insubordinate to an officer.
Or should we excuse the leaders and blame
instead the mass benighting media
of print, radio, movies and TV?
Or is there something about the power
of language that inclines us all to lie?

Chimps can lie, so perhaps living in groups
requires illusions to keep us closed
out from the cold truth that cuts too deep
and separates one from the numberless.
Better a true leader we like who lies
than a Chomsky cocksure philosopher
or solitary bard living for words.
Churchill and FDR had radio,
Hitler his own book and movie deal
with Mein Kampf and The Triumph of the Will.
McCarthy and Kennedy had TV
to twist public wrestling into politics.
By the time of Jackie's gowned Camelot
the art of public deception was glitzed,
and Las Vegas became the capital

of the new lit State of Entertainment—
of the rat pack, mafia, and murders
of Kennedys and Marilyn Monroe.
Washington was only needed to write
the script as the work of lone assassins.

The last century was American,
but it looks like the twenty-first is not.
From Hitler, America received a gift
of fascist Europe's geniuses in flight,
but now we've blown it all away on sports,
computer games, pop music, and cool drugs.
We're back to being boom box kids cruising
at night on empty down a Texan street.
The television dumbing down has brought
us back to the level we were at
with a Know Nothing Party, Scopes Trial,
and public lynchings of radicals and blacks.
Ashcroft intones now just like McCarthy.
Lynne Cheney is making America First!
a dumbing of public education.
For the new century, Earth is tilting
toward tyrannical China with its love
of executions in public stadiums.
With Aids and tribal wars in Africa,
the Middle East becomes the end
of civilization where it began.
Europe's senescent mind now lives within
an American home for assisted living.

Rage on, Ezra, but it's not usura,
you old modernist fake fascist bastard;

and it's not the Jews, Mr. Eliot—
though I would certainly indict Sharon.
Reactionary feudal William Yeats
is truer to the lie of final time,
and it's that proud antithetical gyre
that is now probably screwing us all.
Or could it also be Wallace Stevens'
necessary angel of our ashen earth—
the tragic angel of a new Dark Age.
Between the ancient and the classical
came the archaic Aegean Dark Age.
Between the classical and medieval
arose the Eurasian Gothic Dark Age.
Now between the global and the Gaian
comes the Dark Age of dying religion.
Whatever it is we spend on klieg lights,
American movies are played in the dark.

Jane Toby

62 YEARS OLD
WOODSTOCK, NEW YORK
Worked with Le Donne in Nero, Verona, Italy. Initiated Women in Black in Woodstock.

You Go On With Your Dying (After Mark Strand)

Nothing can stop you.
Not the night. Not the day. Not the sound of your
 breathing.
Not the street out there
Not your house not here.
You go on with your dying.
Nothing can stop you.
Not the nurse who rocks you
Not your baby who cries for you
Not your son you thought would live forever.
Not your mother not here
Not your father in prayer
Nothing can stop you
You go on with your dying.
You lie in your bed and stare at your city
Your city no longer here
the city you thought would last forever.
You lie in your bed and stare at the stars
The stars a blanket of flame.
When you wake at night, wet with blood,
dry of tears,
You go on with your dying.
Nothing can stop you.
Not the women standing in silence

Not the men raising their fists
Not the girls who bathe you in tears
Not the boys who dig ditches for you
Not the doctors who cry out for medicines
Not the medicines not here.
Nothing can stop you.
You go on with your dying.
Not the mistakes of the past
Not the folly of the future
Not the ancient hopes, the old remorse
Nothing can stop you.
You go on with your dying.
You cup your hands over your eyes
and the world goes on without you
The world that stopped as the bombs
rain down
The world that forgot you were human,
The way it felt to be human.
Only you remember:
You go on with your dying.

Chase Twichell

PLANET OF SMOKE AND CLOUD

The earth could not keep
its dead in storage.
Cirrus, stratus, the sky
sloughed off their cloudy migrations.
Tides of wars spilled back and forth
across the phantom boundaries
in the naturalization of dust to dust,
dust the pale colors of human countries.
In a brilliancy of particles
the atoms combined and recombined,
flashing in the grim kinetics
of the earth dispersed
back into its elements,
and with it everything else:
hydrogen, the rippling fires,
our numberless obsessions
with love and power,
all bathed in the spiritual
phosphorus of the afterglow.
Of all the worlds lost
in the hopeless ascendency
of matter toward God,
one was a fluke of aesthetics.
A hand's rayed bones
could be a bird's wing,
inscrutable fossil
locked in a radiant cinder.

Reetika Vazirani
Williamsburg, Virginia
Writer-in-Residence

MOUTH-ORGANS AND DRUMS

fighting   god it shattered belts
a hundred thousand women who
from balconies bowed   palace grounds
bells and shell necklaces we buried
a night   wrists chinking twenty-two
karat come down to drum level
men line the other side of the chawk
rosewater pista badam suntra
green straws bottled drinks horns blow

                  boxing matches everyone is

voting dice games a new parliament
says cowherders and ayahs
will also live in good houses food
will not know radiation's dead
enzyme take your voucher I check
my lipstick dusty arms feet
no sleep in twenty-four
seven red packages over the field

                  I give a ring to the baker

take hints from the fish man's tilted face
seven days as if the city would
marry of course I went forward

all four classes ate from the same
fringe of leaves tinsel wet
fingers dark light no sacrifices peace
in pearls and in rock
peace in the seas' wilderness
in English   Tamil   Trigigna
and in the jetstream of ocean
peace on the SS Warmachine in
god five hundred thousand rose
all flags no one kingdom select

————

Sidney Wade
GAINESVILLE, FLORIDA

Doomsday Verse

In the dying order, they go first,
the little ones. The black empty heads
have decreed it. They are to be married
to the machinery of death and shepherded
by blank-eyed warheads to the altar.
The power of the powerful will not falter.
Democracy and freedom, etc. etc. etc.
Our vehicles possess a raging thirst.

————

Bill Wadsworth

52 YEARS OLD
NEW YORK, NY
Former executive director, the Academy of American Poets.

Bloom's Photograph

In Reykjavík that year the bomb
talks failed, but we survived among
the sweet dead leaves that lay along
the esplanade before Grant's Tomb.

They spiraled into wind-banked heaps
between the benches and the faded
grass; the season escalated
elsewhere, but here the clever hopes

blew lightly down. Safe beside
each other, we were reading James Joyce
when across the street a white Rolls-Royce
pulled up outside a church. A bride

walked out into the light, exalted—
as if the future, gowned in white,
had made a sudden promise in spite
of Reykjavík. This vision, gilt

by autumn light, had interrupted
Molly Bloom's adulteries,
had stopped the fading of the leaves,
until the newlyweds abruptly

went their way. That faded shot
of Mrs. Bloom her husband keeps
adulterates this bride: one sweep
of the wind and the greenest leaf does not

survive. The scene must change. Ulysses
Grant, in the heat of battle, was known
to sit absorbed, cool as stone,
composing letters home to Mrs.

Grant, saying all he privately
believed was going up in smoke.
Puffing on a cigar, he soaked
the fields with blood in Tennessee,

buried his conscience in each glass
of whiskey, and finally told Lee
at Appomattox that victory
was sad—he did "not care to pass

humiliation on"—he lived
without illusions. So grant us all
another cold and golden fall,
and knowledge as to how to leave

the scene. The bride took off her dress
that night while gangs of boys played ball
against the mausoleum wall.
We shut the book on Molly's "Yes."

Anne Waldman

Global Positioning

"The village whitens" means daybreak.
"The price of honey mead" means tax.
"That warms my stomach" means that it irritates
or surprises.
"They shortened him" means they cut off his head.
—from *Griots and Griottes*, Thomas A. Hale

That the shoe fits for the inaugural demonstration should
not surprise you, that you are in an Abraham Lincoln
freespeech mode of wait and wonder, that someone—
a-family-member-perhaps She-Who-Does-Things? walked
into your room last night, that the conversation about "caol"
and "coded" provoked this outburst, that the President
Select said "vulcanize" when he meant to say "galvanize"
and you thought that was a rubber kind of slip, that Big
Business is ruining your hometown, that the family
member perhaps dreamed of later phoned with two ques-
tions, that one of them concerned the discrepancy
between "lore" and "love" because she was confused when
the President Select said "disimprobably," about the
sexlife of his predecessor, and she was glued to a talk show
that wanted you to be confused yet think "their" way, that
you tried to get her to pitch the other question about the
financial mortality of the Roman senate when it was
worrying the question of supremacy, that all you wanted
was a Supreme Court of your own, and that you said that
repeatedly as you marched around the august Roman
building way up in Washington D.C. where they run your

life from, and that what you said doing a witchy kind ofspell-thing was: "this land is mine, this is mine, I am an American, this was always mine, I speak the language, I pay the tax, I want my own Supreme Court."

It was never yours, you never voted properly, it was never easy to read the score from the dugout, that the game is trans-national now, that continental hegenomy is not your game, it never will be it never was, you never were a player, that pensioners are always are looking for empty bottles in the city dump out by the ballpark and never finding them because some of the world is recycling bottles before they get out that far (into the city dump out by the ballpark) and they didn't warn you because you are far from a telephone, and because you never had one you never knew how to stay in touch but it was never the intention of being human to live by honeyed gadgets, that they might never work for you, and the bottle glass breaks easily, it never would hold together for you although you could be found always wandering the sites of waste and want even if you couldn't see the devices that accumulate above your head far above your head you would never need to know that they might pinpoint your exact whereabouts as you wander the sites of waste and want near the city dump out by the glamorous star-studded ballpark, thinking about glass and its antecedents.

—

Connie Wanek

50 YEARS OLD
DULUTH, MINNESOTA
Two books: Bonfire *(1997)* Hartley Field *(2002); poems in* Poetry,
the Atlantic Monthly, Quarterly West, *and many others*

You Say

You say it's so women in Iraq can vote
from the privacy of their graves.

You say it's so the people in Iraq can
hate their leader openly, as we do.

You say it's for democracy in Iraq
such as we have in Florida.

You say don't worry about the children of Baghdad;
 they're not like our children. They
won't make a fuss.

And all the while the grail fills with oil,
the sand is black with oil,
the forehead anointed with oil,
the quill dipped in oil,
the tongue greased with oil,
the prayer written in oil—

written, and set afire.

Cary Waterman

61 years old
St. Paul, Minnesota

Author of three books of poetry. Currently teaching creative writing at Augsburg College.

January 31, 2003

Before sleep, I go out into the January dark afraid of the
    possibility of war.
I look for the raccoon who appeared here two nights ago,
down from her leafy nest to hunt for food in the dark.

There are prints in the new snow: squirrel, human, maybe
    the raccoon.
Under the immense pine tree I leave a piece of chocolate
    cake,
an offering of peace from a country headed for war.

Out on the Iowa prairie, my dying mother-in-law
    prepares for her 95th birthday.
Housebound now, she watches CNN all day long from
    her snug living room.
She's been down this road so many times before, the
    practice of war, the familiarity.

Outside the raccoon snuffles through the dark.

Reed Whittemore

83 YEARS OLD
COLLEGE PARK, MARYLAND
Professor emeritus, University of Maryland; poetry consultant, Library of Congress, 1964–5 and 1984–85, literary editor of the New Republic, *1968-73, editor, furioso, carleton miscellany, delos.*

ON LOOKING THROUGH A PHOTO ALBUM (OF VIET CONG PRISONERS)

These pictures show us a ragged, un-uniformed
    enemy,
Many too old to fight but strong in defiance,
Many frightened, hurt, dazed,
Many despairing,
Some squatting numb and expressionless,
Some dead.

Their captors surround them in big boots.

Note that most of the faces are looking off stage;
They see something unpleasant approaching.
But in this one the dog is too tired to look,
And the woman in front is done looking.
She has seen it, whatever it is, and turned off;
    her eyes
Are not focussed; she dreams
    of no mortgage foreclosure,
    of no missing relief check.

And here is one of mother and child beside
    stretcher,

Looking at corpse,
Presumably daddy.

And one of a tall American sergeant with scholarly
    glasses
Holding foe by scruff of neck.

Then there are pictures of blindfolded females,
And slim males with their heads in sandbags,
    their hands tied behind them,
And fierce youths plotting against us,
And graybeards with sealed lips.
All with tags on them.

I am American, middle-aged, with college degree.
I have been to war, I have studied war.
I know war to be part of man, death part of war,
And cruelty, deprivation, slaughter of innocents
Part,
Visited on both sides.

Yet I am sold out to this enemy; I like his small
    ears.
I am struck by his wide forehead, his high
    cheekbones.
His suppleness pleases me, and his spirit.
When I look at the gun at his chest, the knife
    at his bowels,
I fear for him.
When I see him hung by the heels I am sick.
The griefs that I find in his wrinkles, his
    patience in crossed legs,

The sullen undauntedness issuing from him
Swamp me with traitorous feeling.
Don't I know that this is a war? that this is
   the enemy?

Nancy Willard

Newberry Medalist Nancy Willard is the author of many poems, novels and award-winning children's books.

Victory Gardens

We planted our garden small.
After dinner my mother and I

tidied the beans, watching the apples fall,
while the radio, hid in a melon pile,

counted the deaths in trenches and fields.
The corn, tall as my brother, whose smile

I can hardly remember, pushed out green hands
to my mother like awaited friends.

When he died, she hid in the tall sheaves.
They too were cut down, a battalion

of comforters, yet the next year the leaves
came again. How do such things survive?

cried my mother. We ploughed our grief
under the stubble alive

and tried to imagine that field in France,
very yellow and empty now, the stalks

of wheat pushing quietly out of the earth,
those witnesses and quiet conquerors.

———

C. K. Williams

C. K. Williams won the Pulitzer Prize in 2000.

War

I

I keep rereading an article I found recently about how Mayan scribes,
who also were historians, polemicists, and probably poets as well,
when their side lost a war—not a rare occurrence, apparently,

there having been a number of belligerent kingdoms
constantly struggling for supremacy—would be disgraced and tortured,
their fingers broken and the nails torn out, and then be sacrificed.

Poor things—the reproduction from a glyph shows
three:
one sprawls in slack despair, gingerly cradling his left
hand with his right,
another gazes at his injuries with furious incompre-
hension,

while the last lifts his mutilated fingers to the conquering
warriors
as though to elicit compassion for what's been done to
him: they,
elaborately armored, glowering at one another, don't
bother to look.

II

Like bomber pilots in our day, one might think, with
their radar
and their infallible infrared, who soar, unheard, unseen,
over generalized,
digital targets that mystically ignite, billowing out from
vaporized cores.

Or like the Greek and Trojan gods, when they'd tire of
their creatures,
"flesh ripped by the ruthless bronze," and wander off, or
like the god
we think of as ours, who found mouths for him to speak,
then left.

They fought until nothing remained but rock and dust
and shattered bone,

Troy's walls a waste, the stupendous Meso-American cities abandoned

to devouring jungle, tumbling on themselves like children's blocks.

And we, alone again under an oblivious sky, were quick to learn

how our best construals of divinity, our "Do unto, Love, Don't kill,"

could easily be garbled to canticles of vengeance and battle prayers.

III

Fall's first freshness, strange: the season's ceaseless wheel,

starlings starting south, the leaves annealing, ready to release,

yet still those columns of nothingness rise from their own ruins,

their twisted carcasses of steel and ash still fume, and still,

one by one, tacked up by hopeful lovers, husbands wives, on walls,

in hospitals, the absent faces wait, already tattering, fading, going out.

These things that happen in the particle of time we have to be alive,

these violations which almost more than any altar, ark, or mosque

embody sanctity by enacting so precisely sanctity's desecration.

These broken voices of bereavement asking of us what
    isn't to be given.
These suddenly smudged images of consonance and
    piece.
These fearful burdens to be borne, complicity, contri-
    tion, grief.

——

Eleanor Wilner

65 YEARS OLD
PHILADELPHIA, PENNSYLVANIA
Most recent book, Reversing the Spell: New and Selected Poems.
Teaches in M.F.A. Program for Writers, Warren Wilson College.

Found in the Free Library

"Write as if you lived in an occupied country."
　　　　　　　　　　　　　　　—Edwin Rolfe

And we were made afraid, and being afraid
we made him bigger than he was, a little man
and ignorant, wrapped like a vase of glass
in bubble wrap all his life, who never felt
a single lurch or bump, carried over
the rough surface of other lives like
the spoiled children of the sultans of old
in sedan chairs, on the backs of slaves,
the gold curtains on the chair
pulled shut against the dust and shit

of the road on which the people walked,
over whose heads, he rode, no more aware
than a wave that rattles pebbles on a beach.

And being afraid we forgot to notice
who pulled his golden strings, how
their banks overflowed while
the public coffers emptied, how
they stole our pensions, poured their smoke
into our lungs, how they beat our ploughshares
into swords, sold power to the lords of oil,
closed their fists to crush the children
of Iraq, took the future from our failing grasp
into their hoards, ignored our votes,
broke our treaties with the world,
and when our hungry children cried,
the doctors drugged them so they wouldn't fuss,
and prisons swelled enormously to hold
the desperate sons and daughters of the poor.
To us, they just said war, and war, and war.

For when they saw we were afraid,
how knowingly they played on every fear—
so conned, we scarcely saw their scorn,
hardly noticed as they took our funds, our rights,
and tapped our phones, turned back our clocks,
and then, to quell dissent, they sent. . . .
(but here the document is torn)

Leonore Wilson

44 years old
Napa, California
Leonore is a poet and novelist and college teacher.

Tomoko Uemura is Bathed by Her Mother

photograph by W. Eugene Smith

The small shoulders of Tomoko sprout hands
        like the beginning

        of flowering; the first leaves
on the *Aesculus californica* in February . . .

But this is not beautiful, or meant to be,
        this girl blighted by nuclear fission,

deformed as some might say: a travesty, limbs

        not really human, crooked
as found in the most wild landscapes of the Pacific,

pine-bent, cypress-twisted, but this is not beautiful,
        or meant to be. . . .

And yet the mother whose daughter is stretched
        across her lap like Christ

has that beneficent Mary face as she looks down
        at this one she has created;

she has placed her maternal body naked inside
the bath water too

as if saying I am a part of you, I am

the sponge that absorbs
the outlandish pain, the unimaginable human cross

of what war creates; our bodies are as one
again, as trunk is knitted to branch to twig . . .

your suppurating skin, the sap that sticks to my
flesh, as the colostrum that once

oozed from my breasts, and this water that is taking our
blood,
our chaff, is ours

exchanged

as when I first created you in my womb,
when

you were merely a speck of light,

a light of pure goodness with all the potential

of that goodness, my darling
that I still see in your blinded eyes.

Michael Wolfe

57 years old
Santa Cruz, California
Author of four books of poetry, also fiction, history, and travel, and recently co-producer of a historical documentary film, Muhammad: Legacy of a Prophet, *broadcast nationally on PBS.*

East of New York

For Tamim Ansary

Fifty thousand crickets are talking to the moon.
I'm here doing the translation.
Moon they say, straight to its face
You outflank all Afghanistan this evening,

Grinding the Panjshir Valley underfoot
Without a comment,
Gaining weight, granting nothing
Even to these soldiers laid out in the road.

Who can turn the stars so pale
Or flash a more complacent smile?
Only the two-legged ones match your cool indifference.
Staring up at you they see—a face.

Fighting in the mountains and the valleys,
The columns of the missing keep on growing.
While you, enormous eye,
Go about your business without blinking,

Gaining size as they increase in number,

Crossing the elliptic like a side street,
Blotting Venus, magnifying Mars,
Accompanied by clouds and by our outcry.

---

winnie wong
28 YEARS OLD
BOSTON, MASSACHUSETTS

sanctuary under a palm frond

vincent graduated from high school at age 13.
they said he was a genius and spoke 6 languages who
   never lost a game of chess.

my grandmother stood in line for the tiniest sliver of
   fish, and enough salt to brim two thimbles.

the oatmeal dwindled so they mixed it with yams, which
   grew in the garden, while shells ricocheted off the soil.

their parents spent nights praying to remote gods for
   forgiveness from such common crimes of the heart.

that the children should be spared.
they murmured,
methodically combing the lice
from their soft scalps.

it was a bright, hot morning.
in singapore,
when the shelling began in earnest.

your family fled slipping on sheafs of tropical palm fronds
   and the abandoned belongings of their neighbors.

she said it was like an optical illusion.
the way her youngest brother lay dying in her arms.

Gail Wronsky

46 YEARS OLD
TOPANGA CANYON, CALIFORNIA
I'm the author of five books, including Dying for Beauty *(2000).*

O Alive Who Are Dead

after Marianne Moore

They're fighting in deserts and caves:

we must conquer
in ourselves
what causes war.

Patience, patience, patience:

we must conquer in ourselves what
causes war.

In snow, some on crags, some in
quicksand. Some whom we love,
whom we know—

and woundbearings and bloodshed.
Nothing can be so defeating

as inwardly doing nothing.

Joseph Zaccardi

*I served in Vietnam and wrote a poem about that experience; I think it
touches, in a horrible way, on what is going on today in Washington and
Iraq.*

Search and Rescue

In my journal I write: Rescue.
Today we set out to rescue men
from an LST
run aground in the waters off the
Mekong.
We are not a part of this country.

The first thing I notice is the
whistle
of bullets through leaves, like birds
tearing bits apart.
What are the names of these trees.

The body we find is stripped of
flesh, eyelids
peeled away.
The body is blue and bloated.
It stares at us.
There are no birds in the trees, only rain.

We taste the metal of rain, look
into that face.
Indecent, red curl around glutinous
eyes.
We force ourselves to look at the
hairless
engorged genitals.
Is he one of ours or one of theirs.

Everything about the rescue
is disproportionate. Everything
about the rise
and cry above, pornographic. The
choking roar.
The cover of tracer and fire.

White blooms at the cross of two
rivers.
Helicopters e-vac us to our ship.
Breath
smoking in the reefers. We store
and tag the body.

The sun is brown over the hot
jungle.

I vomit into the cold shaft of the
pallet lift.
Everything until now is a lie.

———

Nina Israel Zucker
Cherry Hill, New Jersey

Shopping List

—Ayat al-Akhras, 18, walked up to this supermarket last
   Friday with a bomb;
Rachel Levy, 17, was carrying a shopping list

I would show her the ground, the mice in the basement,
   those stoic daffodils,
collections of letters tied with rawhide and bells,

or the woman at the back of the church telling me to
   speak louder,
she can't hear and where are the free doughnuts,

or the dream of shuffling papers, not having enough, the
   moments before
you hear from your parents and realize they have no idea

what state you are in, before you pass by the spiny
   headed pineapple,
or the strawberries nestled together like overgrown
   pomegranate seeds

maybe it is learning to wait at 2am, maybe it is a cell
   phone ringing
maybe it is your child telling you a story, his hands, your
   hands

his feet, your feet, he turns his palms up as he talks.
What to buy for dinner seems so simple now—

and what the photographer sees: a girl posed before a
   garden backdrop
hair thick and exposed, modern clothes, familiar expression,
   looking

straight into the camera. I would show it to her, before
   she strapped bombs
to her waist and crossed the boundary. I would tell her
   like Stein, there is
no

there *there*. Maybe in a season like this I would show her
   what can be good.